INSECTS IN FLIGHT

INSECTS IN FLIGHT

JOHN BRACKENBURY

BLANDFORD

A BLANDFORD BOOK

First published in the UK 1992
by Blandford
(A Cassell imprint)
Villiers House
41/47 Strand
London WC2N 5JE

Distributed in the United States
by Sterling Publishing Co., Inc.
387 Park Avenue South, New York, NY 10016-8810

Distributed in Australia
by Capricorn Link (Australia) Pty Ltd
P.O. Box 665, Lane Cove, NSW 2066

British Library Cataloguing-in-Publication Data
A catalogue record for this book is available from
the British Library

ISBN 0-7137-2301-7

Designed by Yvonne Dedman
Typeset by Chapterhouse, The Cloisters, Formby L37 3PX
Printed and bound in Hong Kong
by Dah Hua Printing Co. Ltd.

Half-title page Rear view of a flying mantis.
Frontispiece Large skipper butterfly *Ochlodes venatus*.
Title page Plume moth (family Pterophoridae).
Above and opposite Scorpion fly *Panorpa communis*.

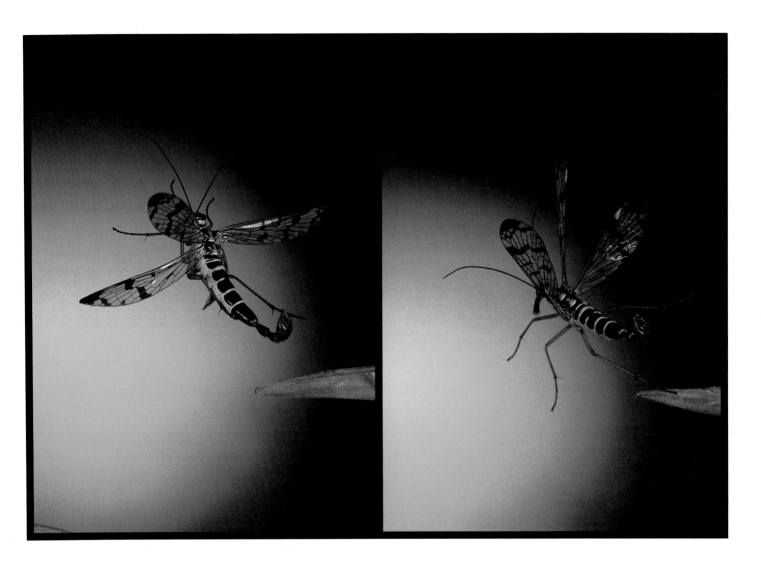

CONTENTS

INTRODUCTION

In April 1987 I made my first springtime visit to the Mediterranean and the experience was unforgettable. Along with a planeload of rather winter-worn fellow travellers I exchanged the demure spires of rural England for the gleaming cupolas of the Greek island of Rhodes. Hillsides wrapped in purple sage and seashores lined with corn marigolds greeted the eye. Never one to use a camera in those days, I bitterly regretted not being able to record my impressions for the benefit of my wife, who couldn't accompany me on the trip.

I returned to England quite dizzy with the vividness of the colours that I had seen. Before long I was again combing through the hedgerows of my usual haunts in search of newly emerging insects. The idea of collecting and preserving insects had never appealed to me, but since childhood I had been fascinated with their habits and behaviour. Now, for some reason that I could not quite fathom, it suddenly seemed a good idea to try to make use of all those accumulated experiences. I suppose the desire must have been prompted by the disappointment that I had earlier felt on missing the opportunity to record those glorious moments on Rhodes.

It did not take me long to decide that the best way for me to put these experiences together was through the story of flight. I also realized that, although I had barely handled a camera in my life, the story would have to be told with the help of pictures. I didn't appreciate what pleasures and headaches would lie in wait for me!

The last four years have turned out to be a voyage of discovery. The camera, this assembly of glass and metal, has provided a window into a different world. There have also been times when patience has been tested to its limits by cantankerous equipment and self-willed beetles and wasps. One episode stands out clearly in my mind.

It happened soon after the project had started. I had been fortunate in recruiting the help of a very capable electronics engineer, Andrew Dack, and by the summer of 1988 we had constructed a prototype system for photographing insects in free flight. Cheered by some initial successes we had with 'home-grown' insects I now felt confident enough to put the system to the test on location in Spain.

I chose the Picos Mountains in the northwestern part of the peninsula, an area which I knew to contain a rich blend of North Atlantic and Mediterranean species. So, having loaded approximately 150 kg of assorted lenses, flash-guns, metal stands, electronic black boxes, laser tubes and heavy-duty car batteries into the back of my twenty-year-old Land Rover, I set out for the ferry that would take me from Portsmouth to Brittany.

A wheel bearing problem that I had unwisely failed to attend to before embarking on the journey meant that I arrived at my destination approximately one thousand miles later with a brain that had been thoroughly addled by the sound of rubber pounding heavily against tarmac. To make matters worse, the magnificent Picos were gloomily hidden in mist and the butterflies that I had expected to find jauntily dancing across the upland meadows were clinging grim-faced and wet from heavily drooping grass stems. This was not an auspicious beginning!

I camped for the night in the beech and oak forests that cloak the lower slopes of the mountains, and next morning prepared to reconnoitre one of the familiar tracks leading up into the mountains from the lovely village of Espinama. I had just squeezed the Land Rover into the tiny car park of the village 'hypermercado' when the owner of a nearby house pointed out to me that the nose of the vehicle was obstructing the entrance to his drive. I put down my rucksack, containing amongst other things my prized Nikon FE2 camera, climbed back into the car and engaged reverse.

1. With a wing span of 120 mm the wood nymph butterfly *Hypermnestra idea* is one of the largest flying insects.

I was still thinking about the mists and that worrying wheel bearing when I felt a soft crunching beneath one of the rear tyres. It was with a feeling of numbness that I got out and confronted my rucksack ingloriously stoved in along the middle like an army cadet's hat. For an irrational moment I even wondered whether a thick woollen jumper, an anorak and a pile of cheese sandwiches might somehow have softened the effect of $1\frac{1}{2}$ tonnes of Land Rover on an expensive camera body.

I tried to ponder the implications of this event. Suddenly 150 kg worth of carefully packed paraphernalia had been rendered redundant, and with it my hopes for this project. This was the first serious test of my resolve, and my immediate thoughts were to catch the next available ferry home out of the port of Santander and possibly ditch the paraphernalia lock, stock and barrel into the Bay of Biscay. But I finally chose to acknowledge the comic, ridiculous irony of the situation, consoling myself that things couldn't possibly get worse.

I will spare the reader most of the details of what followed during the ensuing month. Suffice it to say that even the weight of a Land Rover cannot quite destroy a well-made titanium camera body. Although it was dented in a dozen places, the camera shutter and wind-on facilities miraculously survived intact. I plugged most of the torn metal gashes with plasticine and hoped for the best.

A few weeks later, back in England, I opened box after box of freshly processed transparencies only to find that 90 per cent of them had been fatally over-exposed. I wrathfully re-examined the resurrected Nikon and discovered an unplugged crack less than a hair's breadth in diameter. At this point it would have been easy to write off the whole enterprise as a total disaster. But at least I had gained skill at using the equipment, and, more importantly I now understood much more about the idio-syncrasies of my photographic subjects; this could not be experience wasted. In any case, looking back I doubt whether a single one of the two thousand or more photo-graphs that I had taken would have passed final muster even if they had been perfectly exposed.

The next year, and the year after, I returned to Spain sporting a new camera and a new wheel bearing. In between, I continued to scour the Cambridgeshire hedgerows. The result, after editing nearly twenty thousand photographs, is what you see in this book. My chief aim has been to obtain pictures that will inform, and at the same time, perhaps, inspire people to look a little more closely at the insects that they may see in the garden or during walks in the countryside. The explanatory drawings and diagrams have all been taken directly from original photographic material, so that the book will be self-contained and therefore easier to read and understand. I am aware that many readers may not wish to burden themselves with the technical details of how an insect's wings work, but I hope the pictures will largely speak for themselves. If these readers are tempted to tarry just a moment longer next time they see a glinting dragonfly's wings, the book will have achieved its main objective.

I would like to express my gratitude to the following people who have helped me in various ways during the preparation of this book. Andrew Dack, whom I have already mentioned, and Richard Wang, both engineers, without whose skills my ideas could not have been translated into practical hardware. Rachel Chesterton for the drawings especially commissioned for the work, and Jane Seymour-Shove for spending long hours typing the manuscript. My friend and former colleague Roger Akester, who played no direct part in the project but whose oft-stated conviction that pictures should inform as well as give pleasure I have come to appreciate. Finally, my wife, who bore me through some difficult moments and sat for hours with a projector in a darkened room, helping me to sift the few grains of wheat from the billowing chaff!

2. The benefits of flight are many, but it is also costly on energy and so must be used only where necessary. Moths such as this red underwing are indefatigable fliers, but rely on a steady intake of nectar from flowers to fuel their muscles. Most hours of the day are spent hidden from sight, conserving their energies and, with their sombre coloration, avoiding detection by predators.

· 1 ·

COSTS AND BENEFITS OF FLIGHT

If we ask the question 'Why do animals fly rather than walk or run?' we can think of lots of fairly obvious reasons that could equally apply to people travelling by air. Flight is an effective form of transport because it is fast and it is direct. But in some respects it is also much safer than travelling over the ground. Many potential hazards, distractions and obstacles lie in wait for the unwary walker, and these disappear once an animal has acquired the ability to fly.

Suppose that a bird, say a thrush, and a mammal, such as a hare, both wish to travel from a point A to a point B 1km away. Between these two points lie a woodland copse, an open field and a stretch of river.

Assuming a reasonably favourable wind, the thrush completes the journey quickly and uneventfully, overflying all of these topographical features and avoiding any hazards that might be associated with them. The hare, on the other hand, may be forced to make a lengthy detour around the river and will certainly avoid a straight traverse through the wood. It may have to keep a constant check on its surroundings for signs of predators striking from above (eagles, hawks), below (weasels, stoats) or the side (foxes), not least whilst it is negotiating the open field. On the credit side, the path taken by the hare may also present it with new opportunities for grazing, but in terms of expedience and hazard avoidance the hare on the ground is not in the same league as the thrush in the air.

If you require evidence that flying is safer for animals than walking, bear in mind that most birds that are killed by natural predators fall victim while they are on the ground, not in the air. Also, remember that the albatross, which rarely leaves the air, lives on average much longer than most walking and running animals of a similar size.

Not surprisingly, the tremendous advantages that flight confers upon an animal cannot be achieved without costs. Flight requires enormous structural specialization, and the inevitable counterpart of specialization in one direction is restriction in other directions. Bats, birds and extinct pterodactyls have all had to forfeit the use of the front limbs for any effective role other than locomotion. The backbones of flying vertebrates have also become shorter and stiffer to provide a firm basis for the wings and to prevent 'wobble' in the fuselage during flight. This in turn means loss of flexibility in the spine and the hips: bats are unable to walk but can only crawl feebly on the ground, and when we examine the skeleton of a bird it is quite difficult, anatomically, to see exactly how the creature manages to stand upright on two legs! In fact, the congenital abnormality known as 'kinky back' which cripples domestic chickens results directly from the radical alterations that evolution made to the spine of the poor bird's ancestors in the furtherance of flight!

Insects have taken an entirely different approach to the design of the flight machine, as we shall see in Chapter 2, and it calls for much less of a sacrifice on the rest of the body. But they share with all other flying animals the need to operate with a flight motor that is a very 'heavy burner': the flight muscles of insects, bats and birds consume energy at far greater rates than those of running, walking, burrowing or even swimming animals. To be fair, this particular 'energy penalty' is considerably offset by the fact that flying animals generally move faster than those on the ground and actually use less energy over a given distance. But there is no hiding the fact that flight is expensive on fuel, and this forces flying animals either to concentrate on a high-energy diet or to spend a lot of their time foraging for food. It is noteworthy that many of the most agile fliers, such as hummingbirds, hawkmoths and bees, subsist on a diet of almost pure sugar. This is not only highly calorific but also rapidly absorbed within the gut, and therefore becomes available for use by the muscles practically immediately.

Although flying animals are largely immune from hazards on the ground, they encounter a new set of hazards in the air. Weather, of course, is one of them, particularly the wind. But the effects of wind should not be over-estimated: any well-designed aerial machine, animal or otherwise, can not only cope with powerful air currents but can also turn them to its own advantage. 'Hang-gliders', just like soaring birds, rely on powerful updraughts of air, and modern transatlantic aircraft deliberately seek out high-altitude jetstreams to assist transit.

Seabirds pursuing ocean-going vessels provide a splendid example of the use of air currents to obtain a 'free lift'. A tall ship moving forward at speed leaves behind a region of low air pressure. Close to the stern this produces extremely boisterous eddies, but at the top of the 'turbulence bubble' the current is relatively smooth. It is here that seabirds will receive 'tow' from the ship, enabling them to glide forward along with the stern at speeds of 20 or 30 knots with barely a beat of the wings. A similar manoeuvre is used by racing car drivers when overtaking a rival. The trick is to drive close enough to the rear of the one in front to engage its slipstream. This not only produces an extra drag on the car ahead but also, if performed quickly and correctly, provides a surge of extra power in the car seeking to overtake.

The risks of collision

It might be imagined that one of the main hazards of flight, at least statistically speaking, would be collision with one's own neighbours since the air can be a very congested place. Collisions between flying animals could be potentially far more serious than similar encounters between animals on the ground: if a bird accidentally breaks a wing it is virtually condemned to death by starvation or predation. The consequences of fracturing a limb bone in a ground-living animal are likely to be far less serious. Scientists, naturalists and veterinary surgeons have recorded many instances of terrestrial wild animals showing in their skeletons signs of old breaks that have successfully repaired. Few comparable records exist in the case of birds with broken wings, simply because the bird will not have survived to carry out the repair. A recent survey showed that, of seventy-eight woodcock that had been shot, fifteen had old breaks in various parts of the skeleton, but none of these was in the wings.

Yet this does raise the question 'How can one assess the risk of collision between flying animals?' At first sight the risk would seem to be substantial, considering the flocking tendencies of many species of insect, bird and bat. But this assumption must be weighed against common experience. In many years of birdwatching I have witnessed only one case of accidental collision between birds that resulted in physical damage: two common snipe collided breast-to-breast on take-off and knocked one another unconscious. It was very dramatic at the time, but both recovered and were airborne again within minutes. The experience of other observers may be different, but birds seem to be exceptionally clever at avoiding accidental brushes with their neighbours.

However this does not mean to say that birds scrupulously avoid any kind of physical contact involving the wings: quite the opposite. Male woodpigeons will loudly and violently cuff one another during rival encounters in trees, but evidently the likelihood of suffering a broken bone in these circumstances is far less than during a high-speed impact between those same two birds in flight. And the same goes for butterflies. The fragile appearance of the wings belies the fact that individuals jostling for position on a favourite flower will thrash out violently with their wings to dislodge competitors like wasps and bees.

In the absence of any real statistical data on the incidence of collisions between flying animals, one is inevitably drawn to making comparisons with everyday situations in human activity. How do the risks compare, for instance, between a flock of wading birds wheeling and diving in close formation on the shoreline, and a crowd of rush-hour commuters streaming in all directions in a busy railway station? Or a motorist inching his way forward through a throng of traffic at a busy intersection? But neither of these analogies is quite appropriate, since both involve potential encounters at relatively low speeds.

A more meaningful comparison would perhaps be with aircraft taking off and landing at a major airport. At Heathrow, for instance, which is one of the busiest airports in the world, a take-off or landing occurs roughly every two or three minutes during the day. Flight control ensures that each incoming or outgoing aircraft keeps a distance of some 4–5 km from its neighbour. This minimum 'safe distance' presumably takes into account the size, speed and manoeuvrability of the aircraft as well as the speed of the pilot's reflexes.

How does the flock of birds compare? To take our shoreline waders, the 'safe distance' is at most a few body lengths, even though flight speeds may be well in excess of 30–40 km per hour. Yet has anyone seen two dunlin collide? Perhaps this comparison is unfair to the aircraft. The regulations governing safe distances in commercial flights are obviously much tighter than those operating in, for instance, display teams or military aircraft in combat formation. But these situations are highly stereotyped and exhaustively rehearsed, and bear little real resemblance to the varied and spontaneous flight patterns seen in flocks of birds.

When we consider flying insects, it is virtually impossible even to hazard a guess as to the statistical level of collision between individuals. The subjects are usually so small physically that observation with the naked eye would be totally unreliable. In some instances, such as bees and butterflies visiting the same clump of flowers, the flight path seems to be highly controlled and there is probably a great deal of conscious avoidance of one another. In others, particularly swarming insects, the instinctive drive towards flight in a straight line makes collision almost inevitable.

Fortunately, the tough 'shell' or exoskeleton of insects ensures that they are able to withstand a certain amount of everyday buffeting. If we consider a swarm of locusts taking to flight, the chances of any single individual avoiding collision with its fellows seems remote. But a locust is robustly built, and unless it sustains a blow hard enough to break the leading edge of one of its wings it will eventually succeed in gaining altitude and 'living space'.

Ants taking off from the mouths of their nests at the start of their nuptial flight, and bees passing in and out of the entrances to their hives, provide two further examples of high-density traffic increasing the risks of collision. In these cases naked-eye observation is a somewhat more reliable guide and, as far as bees and wasps are concerned, there seems to be quite a considerable degree of accurate steering both on landing and take-off.

Reflexes and aerobatics

Even better examples of controlled flight in tightly packed situations spring to mind. Take 'winter gnats' (in reality not gnats at all, but small craneflies) rising and falling in their plume-like formations in the lee of hedgerows and garden trees. Many readers must have asked themselves how they avoid colliding with one another. If you try to focus your eyes on a single individual in the column, you may notice that it follows its own independent gyration. It seems impossible that they could all be doing this, and yet still avoid contact, unless there was a high degree of control involved.

Perhaps one of the most exquisite examples of controlled flight is the twirling 'pas-de-deux' performed by courting butter-flies. During this manoeuvre the pair rises straight up into the air, often pursued by supernumerary males, so that four or more individuals will be seen orbiting tightly within a space no larger than an orange. Whether or not the wing tips make brushing contact it is impossible to say, but there is no obvious indication of faltering in their movements. Even if the wings did impact, they are extremely resilient and capable of bending. This is helped by the fact that the margins of the wings of moths and butterflies are usually fringed with hairs; these have an aerodynamic role, but also remove any 'sharp edges'.

For the ultimate in precision flying one must turn to the otherwise rather unalluring bluebottles, greenbottles and houseflies. Many of these insects, when they are not basking lazily on sunlit treetrunks and fence posts, are describing lightning arabesques in the air in playful pursuit of one another. But my own prize goes to a much less familiar fly, the dolichopodid ('long-legged') *Argyra diaphana*: if you take a walk through mixed woodland on a spring day your glance might fall on its silver-furred body darting like raindrops above the moist, shady path.

The machinery that is responsible for producing these at times dazzling displays of aerobatic behaviour must be powerful, but also capable of incredibly fine control. The speed of coordination between the various body senses and the wings of the most agile fliers must be considerably greater than the hand speed shown by skilled sportsmen, aircraft pilots and even the most seasoned electronic games parlour addict.

This discrepancy between insects and men is partly a question of size: nerve signals have much shorter distances to travel in insects than they do in human beings. On top of this, however, there can be little doubt that the eyes and brain of many insects are wired together in a very special way that allows them to detect and respond with lightning speed to invisibly tiny movements of the image across the eye. This must also be the case in birds and bats. Some insight into the logistics of the problem can be gained if we look at the performance of a bat in pursuit of a moth and compare this with two similar human situations: first, a top-class tennis player retrieving a very fast, swerving return from his opponent; second, the computer-controlled guidance of a military missile towards a moving target.

All three situations require the subject (bat, tennis player or computer) to compute the speed and trajectory of two bodies: the subject's own and that of the target. This information, gained from the subject's sensors, must be continuously updated in order to ensure final interception.

Let us take the rocket guidance system first. The problem here is that, although the computer obtains information from an 'eye' that can respond within a fraction of a thousandth of a second, the rocket motor is much more sluggish. As a result the system fails unless it is dealing with a large target moving along a reasonably predictable path.

The eye of a tennis player registers more slowly than an electronic photocell, but a good sportsman also relies on experience gained from numerous similar situations encountered in the past. He will use this experience to predict where the opponent's ball is likely to land, taking into account the speed and direction of movement of the opponent's racket as he delivers the stroke. Moreover, the athlete has much finer control over his muscles than the computer has over the mechanical guidance of the missile. In fact a very experienced tennis player could probably intercept his target with two main computations: one as he sets off on his path towards the ball, and a second just before the racket makes contact with the ball. In between he will have integrated all the previously available data on the ball's trajectory and therefore knows more or less exactly how many strides will be needed to reach the target and in what position each part of his body should be at the time. The second computation is mainly a fine tuning, making sure that the precise forces are applied to the ball at the critical moment of impact.

The bat in pursuit of the moth has to cope with the worst of both worlds: the target is moving very fast, and its path is completely unpredictable. From the point of view of the moth, both speed and unpredictability are necessary since neither would alone be sufficient to ensure escape. Anyone who has tried to catch a pet rabbit which has escaped from its run will know that, although the rabbit may not be able to run very fast, the fact that it keeps changing direction makes it a very slippery customer! If the bat is to catch the moth, it must possess not only a highly sensitive detection system and a responsive flight motor, but also a brain that is capable of updating information very quickly. What makes the bat's situation even more difficult is that the quarry is often equipped to the same level of sophistication, and is continually trying to frustrate the hunter by erratic behaviour.

Evasive behaviour in response to bats is found not only in moths. Green lacewings and mantids also use the strategy of sudden unpredictable changes in flight pattern to avoid bat attacks. The element of unpredictability is essential, since the flight speed of these insects is less than 7 km per hour whilst that of the bat may be up to 25 km per hour. Moths, green lacewings and mantids instinctively dive as soon as they detect the ultrasonic beam from an approaching bat. Lacewings simply fold their wings and dive passively through the air. Moths dive passively but also perform powered dives, spirals and swift turns. Curiously, mantids only seem to respond evasively to ultrasound when they are in the air. On the ground they seem oblivious to approaching bats and therefore present a potentially easy target. The reason for this 'flight-gated' behavioural pattern in mantids is not known.

3. In this front view of a soldier beetle *Cantharis* at the point of take-off into flight we see the sternal plates which form the basal elements of the thorax. Lying above the sternal plates are the pleural plates that form the sides of the thorax and underpin the base of the wings. The pleural wing process which forms the main pivot point between the wing and the thorax can be seen just behind the insect's right middle leg. These features are illustrated in greater detail in Figure 5 on page 20.

· 2 ·

THE MACHINERY OF FLYING

In Chapter 1 I attempted to give some idea of the qualities that a flying animal needs in order to control the very powerful flight motor which it has at its disposal. Chapter 2 is concerned with the structure of the flight motor and the way it works. But before delving into the details of the insect flight machine it will be useful to pave the way by looking at flight in bats and birds.

It is much easier to gain an intuitive feel of the way in which birds and bats fly because, apart from some remarkable differences in birds, we can identify almost every bone in our own bodies with a similar bone in the

bat's or bird's body, right down to the fingers and toes. If you peered far enough back into the embryonic period of development it would be evident that, up to a certain age, birds, bats and human beings are indistinguishable from one another, since their bodies are all constructed from the same blueprint. All early embryos in vertebrates show five fingers and five toes, and it is only at a relatively late stage that deletions occur in the bird so that when it hatches it is left with only three fingers, which already carry the buds of the primary flight feathers, and four toes. Bats and humans retain the full complement of fingers and toes, though they deploy them in entirely different ways from one another.

In view of these structural affinities between bats, birds and humans it should come as no surprise that we can easily and accurately duplicate the movements of a bird's or bat's wing using our own arms and shoulders. But to carry out this exercise properly, we must pay attention to the details. Flapping your arms from the elbow would be a complete misrepresentation. The power of an animal's wings comes, not from the wings themselves, but from the breast. This means that the wings are moved from the shoulder.

In order to simulate the movements of a bird's wings you should hold your arms straight out in front of you, level with the shoulders, and palms facing inwards. If you now tense the breast muscles and draw the arms together, then tense the muscles of the shoulder blade to draw the arms apart, you will be making a passable imitation of the flight machine of a bird or a bat. The main difference is that, in proportion to the rest of its body, the breast muscles of a bird or bat are ten to twenty times bigger than our own.

Incidentally, if we ever did discover an alien world where men could fly using their arms as wings, they would probably be weighed down by a keel protruding half a metre from their breastbone and extending down to the crotch. This would be the logical consequence of the way in which vertebrates specialize themselves for flight: nothing less would suffice to attach the enormous bulk of muscle that would be required. Clearly there is a logical paradox here: the hypothetical 'bird-man' would be so heavy that he would never get off the ground. However, if the force of gravity on the alien world were only, say, one-sixth of what it is on earth, the possibilities would look more promising!

How the wings are driven
The flight machine of insects, like almost everything else in their bodies, is built on an entirely different plan from vertebrates. Take the skeleton: every animal requires support in the form of a framework to which the rest of the organs can be attached. Whereas our skeleton consists of bones lying on the inside, covered with flesh (called an endo-skeleton), the skeleton of an insect consists of tough plates lying on the outside, surrounding the muscle and organs (known as an exoskeleton). In structural terms it is like the difference between a chandelier and a Chinese lantern. Or, more appositely, the exoskeleton of an insect fits together more like a suit of armour than a system of articulated rods. Reference to our own bodies therefore offers no intuitive clues towards understanding how the insect flight machine functions. Although the main facts of this mechanism have now been known for decades and have been described many times in textbooks of entomology, it is easy to forget what an extraordinary stroke of imagination it must have required on the part of those naturalists who first devised the keys to work out its complexities.

A simple experiment, which the reader can perform for himself, provides one of the most important clues to the way in which an insect moves its wings. Take a recently killed fly that is still soft and pliable and tap gently with the point of a pencil on the top of its humped thorax. This is the part of the insect's body lying behind the head and carrying the wings and the three pairs of legs. You may find that with each tap the wings move up and down once. Now, instead of tapping, press gently down with the pencil, then release the pressure. You may see the wings rise, then fall.

Two important conclusions can be drawn. First, the wings move not directly, but indirectly (you do not need to touch the wings themselves to make them move). Second, the wing base must be articulated to the top plate of the thorax, movements of which cause the wing to be levered up and down. With the benefit of this practical demonstration, we are now in a position to understand the details of the flight mechanism, helped by the diagrams shown in Figures 1–7 and photographs 3–7 in this chapter.

An insect's thorax is composed of three segments, the second and third of which bear the wings. The wall of each segment is made up of a base plate (sternal plate), two side plates (pleural plates) and the top plate (tergal plate), the whole making up the four sides of a box section. Each wing can be thought of as a double, shelf-like outgrowth from the top and side plates where these two meet to form the top edge of the box.

In fact this is precisely the way in which the wings develop in a young insect, and explains how the wing is a double membrane. The veins, which give structural support to the adult wing, originate as tracheal tubes growing out from the body cavity and intruding between the opposed membranes. In the adult the veins remain connected to the body cavity and continue to receive a supply of nerves and blood to nourish the main fabric of the wing and the various sense organs arranged over its surface. The membranes of the immature wing are rather soft, to allow for its growth and expansion, but once fully formed they harden to present a more resilient surface to the forces generated by the wind. Only the basal attachment remains soft and flexible in order to permit the up-and-down movements that it undergoes during flight.

Embedded within the flexible base of the wing is a series of harder, seed-like elements, called basal sclerites, that enable the wing to pivot upon a peg-like outgrowth from the pleural plate. The basal sclerites also provide attachment points for a series of small muscles that can alter the angle of attack adopted by the wing during flight.

If we now recall the experiment with the pencil, we can see that it is the upward and downward displacements of the tergal plate that cause the wings to rock upon the pivot. The tergal plate is driven by two sets of muscles located within the thoracic segments. In very powerful fliers, these muscles virtually fill the thoracic cavity.

The 'dorsoventral muscles' attach directly to the underside of the tergal plate, span the entire depth of the thorax, then reattach to the sternal plate. Impulses delivered to these muscles from the central nervous system cause them to contract and pull down the tergal plate, therefore indirectly levering up the wing on the pleural pivot.

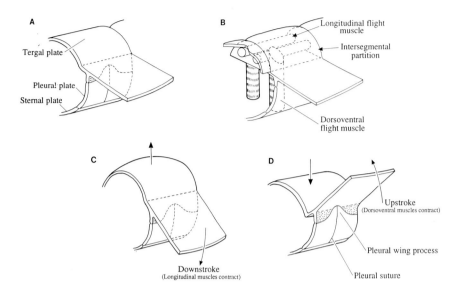

Figure 1. Scheme of the mechanism of wing movement in insects. The diagram shows a single wing-bearing segment of the thorax made up of tergal, sternal and pleural plates. The pleural plate contains the wing process on which the base of the wing rocks up and down as a result of the pulsatile movements of the tergal plate. In **A** and **B** the wing is shown in an intermediate position. **B** shows the two main groups of muscles which act upon the tergal plate. When the longitudinal muscles contract the tergal plate buckles upward, as in **C,** and the wing is forced down. Contraction of the dorsoventral muscles levers the wing upward on the pleural wing process, as in **D.**

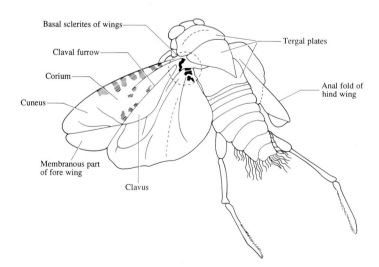

Figure 2. The backswimmer *Notonecta maculata* in flight, drawn from photograph 4. The tergal plates of the first (prothoracic), second (mesothoracic) and third (metathoracic) segments are identified. Small movements of the mesothoracic and metathoracic tergal plates produce upward and downward levering of the wing, which is articulated to the plates via a series of basal sclerites.

4. This rear view of a backswimmer *Notonecta maculata* leaping into flight allows us to see the toughened plate-like elements that form the upper part of the wall of the thorax. The wings articulate with these tergal plates through a series of tiny elements embedded in the wing base, the basal sclerites. Slight in-and-out movements of the tergal plate, under the action of the flight muscles housed within the thorax, are transmitted to the wing base, causing it to lever up and down. Note also the triangular flap on the trailing edge of the fore wing overlapping the leading edge of the hind wing. This claval lobe provides a physical coupling between the two wings during flight. Further details of the different parts of the wing are shown in Figure 2.

The second set of muscles, responsible for producing the downstroke of the wing, stretch longitudinally between the partitions that divide off the thoracic segments from one another. Contraction of these 'longitudinal' muscles causes the two wing-bearing segments to shorten very slightly, making the tergal plates buckle upwards and pivoting the wing downwards.

In a flying insect these pivoting movements are taking place at rates of up to hundreds of cycles per second and the potential for wear and tear is enormous. This is why there are so many elastic, rubber-like elements in the flexible wing base. These absorb the repeated shocks and reduce the frictional stresses in the same way that the rubber mounts of a car engine buffer the chassis

5. A male great green bush-cricket *Tettigonia viridissima* leaping into flight displays its strap-like fore wings and membranous hind wings. Note the domed tergal plates of the wing-bearing segments, articulating with the wing bases. The rear part of the base of the fore wing is modified in male bush crickets to form a sound-producing organ. During the process of stridulation the wing bases are rubbed rapidly back and forth against each other to produce the sound. Details of the tergal plates and wing attachments are shown in Figure 3.

Figure 3. The great green bush-cricket *Tettigonia viridissima* in flight, drawn from photograph 5 to show details of the articulation between the wings and the tergal plates of the thorax.

6. The motion of the hind wings of this *Strangalia* beetle (opposite) has been frozen just at the point where they have made contact above the body at the end of the upstroke. This leaves a clear view of the articulation of the wings with the thorax. Details of this articulation are shown in Figure 4.

Figure 4. This drawing of the beetle *Strangalia* in flight, taken directly from photograph 6, shows the way in which the base of the leading edge of the hind wing articulates via the basal sclerites to the wing process. The basal sclerites are embedded within the soft cuticle forming the flexible joint between the wing and the body. The sternal plates form the basal elements of the thoracic cage. The tergal plates, forming the top armoury of the thorax, are hidden from view by the raised wings.

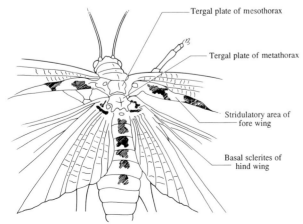

Tergal plate of mesothorax

Tergal plate of metathorax

Stridulatory area of fore wing

Basal sclerites of hind wing

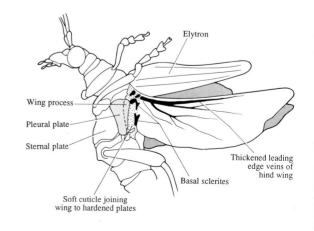

Elytron

Wing process

Pleural plate

Sternal plate

Thickened leading edge veins of hind wing

Basal sclerites

Soft cuticle joining wing to hardened plates

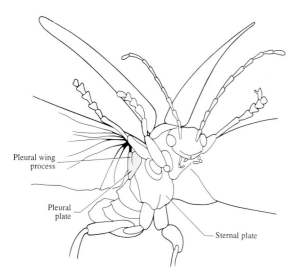

Figure 5. A flying soldier beetle *Cantharis* drawn from the photograph 3 (page 14) to show the pleural and sternal plates that form the sides and bottom of the thorax respectively. The thickened veins near the costal or front margin of the wing form the main leading edge spar. The base of the spar articulates with the thorax via the pleural wing process. The wing process acts as a pivot upon which the wing can be rocked up and down by the movements of the tergal plates.

against the vibrational shocks from the running motor. The wing pivot must also be suitably braced to withstand the high-frequency compressional loading placed upon it by the tergal plate: a 'flying buttress' of toughened chitin (the material out of which exoskeleton is made) spans the body cavity from the pivot to the sternal plate. The line of the buttress can be traced on the outside of the body by a line or suture passing from the pivot down to the base of the leg: this suture is clearly visible, even in photographs of flying insects such as the Egyptian grasshopper in photograph 7.

Although the description given so far suggests that the thoracic plates are driven in a direct push-and-pull manner by the flight muscles, the situation is a little more complicated in practice. Insects would not be the creatures that they are if they did not constantly surprise us by their inventiveness, as we can see if we examine the upstroke phase of the flight movement rather more closely.

7. This side view of an adult Egyptian grasshopper (opposite) *Anacridium aegyptium* leaping into flight shows the pleural and sternal plates that make up the sides and base of the thorax. Both wing pairs are at the summit of the stroke and are about to begin their descent. The trailing edges of the pleated, sail-like hind wing are in contact and are about to peel apart as the leading edge starts its downward movement. Further details of the structure of the thorax and wing base are given in Figure 6.

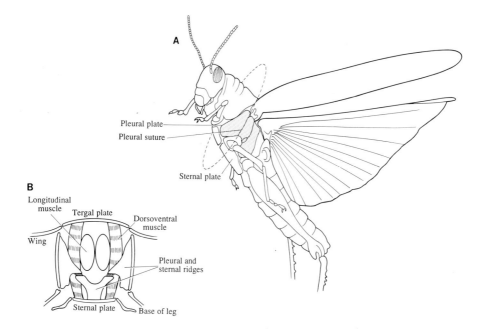

Figure 6. An Egyptian grasshopper *Anacridium aegyptium* in flight, drawn from photograph 7 to illustrate the pleural and sternal plates that form the sides and bottom of the thorax respectively. Each pleural plate has inscribed upon it a line or suture that runs from the wing process to the base of the leg. The suture marks the position of an internal strut of thickened cuticle. The inset shows a diagrammatic cross-section of the thorax at the level of the pleural suture, and includes the flight muscles. Contraction of the dorsoventral muscles pulls down the tergal plate and pivots the wing upwards on the pleural process. The pleural and sternal ridges form a strut that buttresses the wing process against the bottom of the thorax, preventing any compression of the walls as the muscles contract, but allowing them to buckle slightly outwards.

As the tergal plate is pulled down by the dorsoventral muscles it raises the wings, as we have seen, but it also forces the pleural plate to bow outwards. This is because of the geometry of the wing base and its articulation with the tergal and pleural plates, as shown in Figure 7. The pleural plate bows out only slightly, but it is sufficient to make the plate store elastic energy. The wall continues to deform, and to accumulate elastic energy under the strain, until a critical point is reached in the downward movement of the tergal plate. At this point the stretched pleural plate suddenly jumps back, releasing all its elastic strain energy and driving the wing upwards at high velocity.

As a result of this click mechanism, as it is called, the flight muscles can release their energy much more explosively than they would otherwise be able to do. This translates directly into a greater speed of wing movement, and a greater effectiveness at generating aerodynamic lift.

A good idea of how the click mechanism works can be gained by comparing it with the familiar press-stud used in dressmaking. Imagine that the stud is the insect's tergal plate and that the rim of the eye into which the stud is pressed is the pleural plate. Your finger pressing down on the stud represents the force generated by the dorsoventral flight muscles pulling on the tergal plate. As you press the stud, the rim of the eye is forced open until a critical point is reached when the rim suddenly recoils and the stud is snapped home. In the insect, a second click occurs during the downstroke phase of the wings in exactly the same way, except that this time the power is delivered from the longitudinal muscles. This is equivalent to removing the stud from the eye.

The click mechanism has been evolved in order to overcome the inbuilt limitations of living muscle. Insect flight muscle can only contract at rates of up to about one hundred cycles per second. But many insects need to vibrate their wings at much higher rates than this, simply to generate the forces necessary to maintain their bodies in the air. The high-pitched whine of a mosquito's wings tells us that the wings are beating at several hundreds of cycles per second. Insects are able to achieve these very high contraction rates by making the muscles work in tandem with the elastic elements within the thoracic wall.

Patterns of wing beat

The muscles housed in the thorax represent the power plant for flight, and provide for the basic up-and-down movements of the wings, but high-speed photographs of flying insects show that the path traced out by the

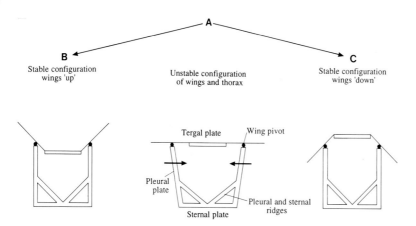

Figure 7. Diagram of the click mechanism of the thorax and wings. The drawings represent a cross-section through the walls of one wing-bearing segment. In **A** the wings are held in an intermediate position between the stroke extremes. This position is unstable because the horizontal distance between the wing pivots is greater than the width of the thorax. This means that the thoracic walls are being pushed outwards by the tergal plate and exert a back pressure on the wing pivots. Recoil of the elastic walls will force the wing to snap either up or down towards one of the stable positions, **B** or **C.**

B

A

8. This longhorn beetle *Leptura rubra* is hovering slowly forward. The photographs were taken when the wings had reached the end of the upstroke (**A**) and the downstroke (**B**) respectively. By drawing an imaginary line between the wing tip positions, we see that the stroke plane is almost horizontal, even though the body axis is held at about 45 degrees. The horizontal stroke plane allows the beetle to produce a maximum vertical lifting force. In **A** the hind wings are in contact and about to peel apart. In **B** the wings have rotated into the characteristic nose-down position (pronation) adopted during the downstroke.

Careful comparison of this photograph with the photograph 6 and with Figure 4 will enable identification to be made of the pleural and sternal plates of the metathorax, and the pleural wing process of the hind wing. Note that in beetles the shell-like fore wings or elytra remain stationary during flight.

A

B

wing is rarely straight up and down at right-angles to the body. Usually the wings are moved in a plane which is inclined at an angle to the body axis, the so-called stroke plane. At the end of the upstroke the wings come to lie above the body and point back-wards, whereas at the end of the downstroke they lie beneath the body and point for-wards. These two points are referred to as the stroke extremes, or points of stroke reversal. During the downstroke the wings therefore sweep downwards and forwards; during the upstroke they sweep upwards and backwards.

The angle of the stoke plane is not fixed but can be altered according to the insect's requirements by the muscles inserting on to the sclerites in the wing base. When an insect is hovering, for instance, the stroke plane is almost horizontal so that the wings can force the air vertically downwards. If the insect now moves forwards, it tilts the stroke

plane forwards so that the air can now be forced both backwards and downwards. The backward and downward components of the air current provide the forces of thrust, driving the insect forward, and lift, keeping its body level in the air.

If you were able to view the wings of a hovering insect in slow motion from the side of the body, you would see the tips moving along a path that had the shape of an ellipse. The long axis of the ellipse is aligned exactly with the inclined stroke plane, and the ends of the ellipse coincide with the two stroke extremes. As an insect moves forward, the path drawn out in the air by the wing tips becomes influenced by its speed of move-ment. The path is no longer a closed ellipse but becomes drawn out into a series of saw teeth, each tooth representing a single wing beat. The shorter, steeper side of each tooth coincides with the upstroke because that is when the wing is moving backwards with

9. The tiny tortoise beetle *Cassida sanguinolenta* launches forward and upward into flight. The wings are shown in their extreme positions at the top of the upstroke (**A**) and the bottom of the downstroke (**B**) respectively. The stroke plane of the wing is tilted forward to enable a horizontal propulsive force to be generated in addition to the vertical lifting force.

respect to the body, and therefore its speed relative to the ground slows down. In contrast, during the downstroke the wing is being moved forwards and its speed combines with the speed of the body as a whole so that the wing tip path is drawn out to form the longer, shallower side of the tooth.

The geometrical consequences of this are important, because it means that the wings of an insect flying forwards must be moving through the air faster during the downstroke than they are during the upstroke. If the angle of attack of the wing did not alter between the strokes, more lift would be generated during the downstroke. This would not necessarily be to the insect's advantage, because it would produce a tendency for the body to bob up and down between the two phases of the stroke. Also, as the reader will appreciate, it means that if the insect is hovering, or moving forwards only very slowly, the wing will be moving

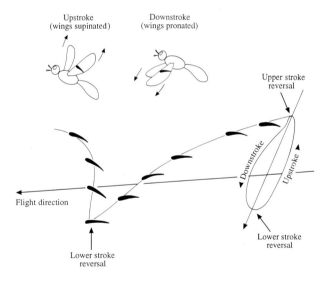

Figure 8. Diagram of the path traced out by the wing tips during the flight cycle. The closed loop on the right-hand side is the path traced out by the wing tip with respect to the body and is the path that would be 'seen' by an observer travelling at the same speed as the insect, or by a stationary observer watching a hovering insect. The line stretching out to the left is the wing tip path with respect to the ground, and is the path that would be 'seen' by a stationary observer as the insect flew past. The diagram also shows how the angle of attack of the wing is altered by rotating the wing 'nose-down' on the downstroke (pronation) and 'nose-up' on the upstroke (supination).

backwards through the air during the upstroke. This will produce a force on the upperside of the wing pushing downwards, not upwards: in other words, negative lift, causing the wings to stall.

Insects get round this problem by altering the angle of attack of the wings so that it is greater during the upstroke. In the case of the insect flying slowly forwards, the wing can now generate an equal lifting force to that produced during the downstroke, even though it is moving through the air more slowly. These changes in the angle of attack are controlled by the small muscles inserting on to the basal sclerites of the wing. A group attached to the forward section of the wing base pulls down the leading edge as the downstroke begins, securing the required reduction in the angle of attack. A second group acting on the rear part of the base has the opposite effect, pulling down the trailing edge at the start of the upstroke and increasing the angle of attack. The whole surface of the wing thus becomes twisted forward, then backwards, during each stroke.

It sounds quite complicated, but you can easily duplicate these movements using your own arms and wrists. Extend your arms to the side, level with your shoulders. Position your hands so that the palms point forwards an an angle of 45 degrees: this represents the notional angle of attack of the wing. Using your pectoral muscles, now draw your arms forwards, keeping them level but at the same time twisting your wrists forwards and decreasing the 'angle of attack' of your hands. This downward twisting movement of the insect's wings is referred to as 'pronation'. Now draw your arms backwards, again keeping them level with your shoulders, but this time twisting the wrists backwards as well: this produces the appropriate increase in the angle of attack of the hand, and is referred to as 'supination'.

You will notice that, if the hand is to continue to supply an upward lifting force during the simulated upstroke, it will have to be twisted right on to its back, that is, palm-upwards. This is precisely what happens in the case of hovering insects and birds: the

10. Plume moths (family Pterophoridae) have a rather slow, hover-like flight and beat their wings in an almost horizontal plane. This can be seen by comparing the positions of the wing tips at the end of the upstroke (**A**) and the downstroke (**B**).

A

B ▶

A

B

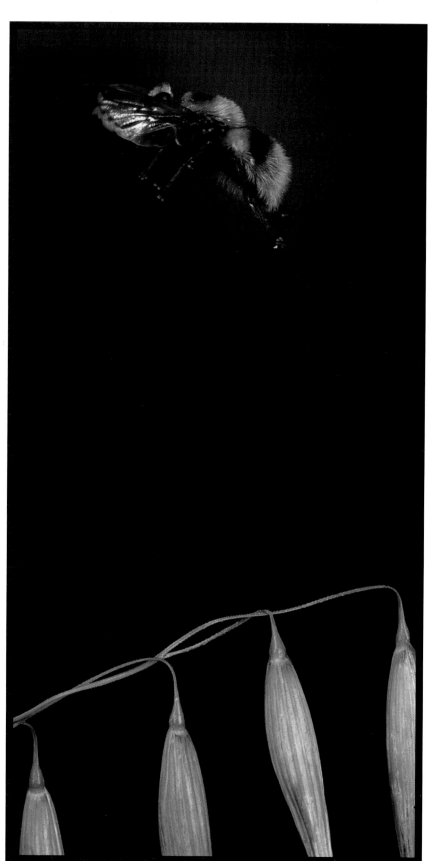

11. The wings of true flies or Diptera beat downwards and forwards at an angle to the body. In **A,** the wings of this hoverfly are poised at the beginning of the downstroke. In **B,** the wing tips of the hoverfly *Volucella bombylans* have come together in front of the head at the end of the downstroke.

wing is twisted upside down during the up-stroke so that it presents the same positive angle of attack to the oncoming air.

In reality, relatively few insects are capable of true stationary hovering, although many operate at very low forward air speeds and are effectively hovering in the sense that they need to twist their wings back and forth in the manner just described. But what happens when an insect flies forward at very high speed?

Now, for each beat of the wings the body has moved forward through a relatively large distance relative to the ground. If we look at the wing tip path, the saw tooth has become stretched out to a shallow ripple. In fact, the wing tip path of a fast-flying insect is practically a straight line: the wing moves through the air at virtually the same speed during both phases of the stroke and there is no need for wing twisting. But it also means that, at these relatively high speeds, most of the airflow over the wing surfaces is due to the forward motion of the body, not to the beating of the wings. Since it is this airflow over the wings that produces lift, this is a very important result because it predicts that as an insect flies faster, its wings do not need to work as hard.

The situation seems too good to be true, and of course there is a catch. The catch is the air resistance which produces the 'drag' on the wing. As an insect flies faster, it is true that it requires less power to sustain the necessary airflow across its wings. But at the same time more and more of the available power in the wing muscles is used in overcoming the effects of viscous drag, caused by the air 'sticking' to the surfaces of the wing and body. As a result there is a practical upper limit to the flight speeds that can be attained, which in each species will depend on the power available within the flight muscles.

Insects and birds

We have spent quite a time considering the ways in which insects deal with the mechanical problems associated with flapping flight. At this point it will be useful to put these findings into a broader context by comparing them with what happens in birds.

In most birds the downstroke is the main power stroke, a fact clearly reflected in the much greater size and mass of the pectoral muscles compared with the muscles that produce the upstroke. There are some exceptions: hummingbirds, like hovering insects, produce equal amounts of lift during the upstroke and the downstroke, and not surprisingly the two sets of muscles are of roughly the same size. Birds also resemble insects in having a series of smaller muscles attached to the base of the wing (in this case the head of the humerus), which can twist the wing surface backwards and forwards, thereby varying its angle of attack.

Careful examination of high-speed motion pictures of flapping bird wings shows that, as in insects, the wing is pronated during the downstroke and supinated during the upstroke. But often the most outstanding feature is the amount of length change taking place within the wing throughout the cycle.

This is one of the most important advantages that birds have over their insect

12. These photographs of the hoverfly *Chrysotoxum cautum* (**A**) and the greenbottle *Lucilia* (**B**) were taken just as the insects were launching into flight. During take-off the wings are beaten in an almost horizontal stroke plane to achieve maximum upward force. The photographs show the wings flung into their maximum forward position in front of the head, at the end of the downstroke.

A

B

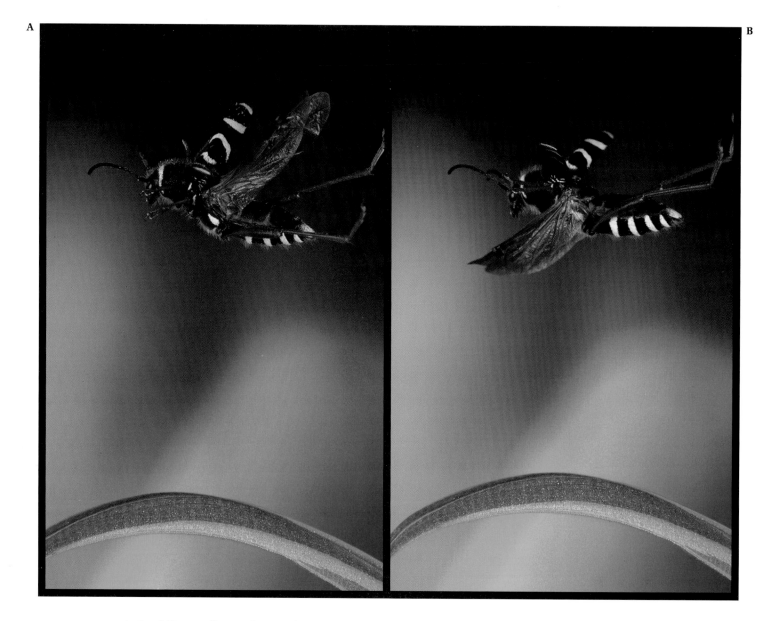

A

B

counterparts: their ability to flex and extend their wings, and of course this results from the fact that the bird's wing is a jointed structure. Flexion and extension can occur at all three main joints: shoulder, elbow and wrist. With these movements a bird is able to vary the surface area of its wings, inducing subtle changes in their aerodynamic performance. For instance, during the upstroke the wing is not only supinated but also drawn in towards the body by flexure of all three joints. This 'feathering' of the wing reduces its resistance as it moves through the air during the recovery stroke, and also minimizes negative lift generation.

A graphic demonstration of the importance of being able to alter the lifting characteristics of the wing through changes in its surface area can be seen in birds soaring into a head wind. Good examples are provided by seagulls or even buzzards soaring motionlessly above headlands, terns hovering close to the surface of the sea before diving for a catch, and kestrels hovering in the breeze rising above a hedgerow.

In the last two cases in particular, the bird's objective is to hold a stationary position with respect to a point almost immediately below the body. The bird must maintain an absolutely steady lifting force in

13. This wasp beetle *Clytus arietis* is photographed in forward flight. Comparing the wing tip positions at the end of the upstroke (**A**) and the end of the downstroke (**B**) respectively demonstrates that the angle of the stroke plane is approximately 45 degrees to the horizontal.

A

14. As the wings approach the bottom of the downstroke they rotate from a 'nose-down' to a 'nose-up' position in preparation for the next upstroke. In these rear views of the longhorn beetle *Agapanthea villosoviridescens* (**A**) and the cardinal beetle *Pyrochroa coccinea* (**B**) the wings have just rotated so that their leading edges face outwards and their trailing edges face inwards.

B

the face of air currents that may be constantly fluctuating. These fluctuations are compensated for mainly by altering the angle of attack of the wings, but also by making tiny adjustments of wing area through flexion and extension of the wing joints.

Insects lack any such provision for altering wing area and most species would be unable to cope with these demanding conditions, although there is one possible exception that springs to mind. In the Pyrenean mountains I have seen mature, fully-winged alpine grasshoppers leaping into the face of high winds rising over a col and succeeding in holding a hovering position for several seconds. This flight pattern is probably part of their normal migratory behaviour, although on this occasion the majority of individuals were unable to make any headway into the wind and fell back into the lee of the col. It is worth mentioning that grasshoppers and their allies are amongst the few insects that possess a pleated hind wing, allowing alterations in surface area. Of course I have no direct evidence that the individuals in the example quoted were using this facility in the same way that hovering birds do.

The other great advantage that birds have over insects in terms of flight control is the possession of a tail. Operating like a fan, the tail is capable of infinite variations in surface area, serving both as a rudder and as an additional lifting surface. Tail-like expansions are found in some larval insects, notably the tail gills of mayfly nymphs, and these also double as organs of propulsion. However, I can think of no example of an insect that employs a similar appendage as a rudder during flight.

Earlier in this chapter we saw that the part of the insect's flight machinery that bears most of the strain developed by the wing muscles is the wing pivot. Consequently the pivot needs to be especially buttressed to undertake its role. A flying bird faces the same problem in its shoulder joint, but the solution which it adopts is quite different.

Once again we can arrive at a better understanding of the problem if we use our

A

B

15. As the wings approach the top of the upstroke they rotate from a 'nose-up' to a 'nose-down' position, in preparation for the next downstroke. These rotations are illustrated here in the ichneumon fly *Netelia* (**A, B**) and the common wasp *Vespula vulgaris* (**C, D,** opposite). In **A** and **C** the leading edges of the wings are approaching the mid-line ahead of the trailing edges and have almost made contact. Fractionally later, in **B** and **D,** the wings have pronated, swinging the trailing edges into contact so that the hind wings can perform a peel at the start of the downstroke.

own arms as a model of the bird's wings. We saw earlier that drawing the outstretched arms inwards with the pectoral muscles duplicates the power stroke of the wings. If you glance down at your shoulder as you perform this movement you will see that the only structure preventing your shoulder joint from collapsing towards your breast bone is the collar bone, which acts as a strut between the two points.

The bird's pectoral muscles are very much bigger and exert much greater stress on the shoulder joint than your pectoral muscles are capable of doing, so you can imagine that a collar bone, scaled down to the size of the bird, would hardly be an adequate brace. To overcome this weakness, birds have developed two 'collar bones'. One of them, the true clavicle or 'wish bone', is rather slender, and most of the load bearing has to be undertaken by a much squatter, pillar-like bone, the coracoid. We humans also possess

a coracoid, but only in vestigial form as a tiny projection on the summit of the shoulder.

The power plant for flight

No review of the machinery of flight would be complete without looking inside the power plant that supplies the energy needed to make the machine run. The power plant, of course, lies within the flight muscles, which are specialized for converting the chemical energy which is obtained from food into the mechanical energy of muscular contraction.

At the microscopic level there is little to distinguish the structure of an insect's flight muscle from that of a bird or a bat. They are all made of the same biological materials and, when activated, a gramme of insect flight muscle and a gramme of bird pectoral muscle both deliver approximately the same force with each contraction.

16. Four consecutive stages in the complete wing beat cycle of the sand wasp *Ammophila sabulosa*. The insect is performing slow forward flight using an almost horizontal stroke plane. The sequence begins in **A** with the coupled fore and hind wings raised above the body at the start of the downstroke. In **B** the wings are pronated and moving downwards and forwards. In **C** the wings have reached the bottom of the downstroke and the fore wing has begun to supinate. In **D** both wings have now supinated and are moving backwards in an upside down position. Comparing positions **B** and **D,** we see that even though the wings are moving in opposite directions (forward in **B** and backward in **D**) they present the same angle of attack to the air. As a result lift is produced equally during the downstroke and the upstroke.

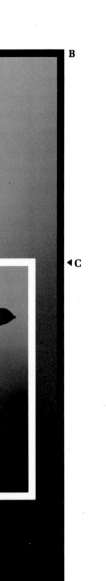

A  B

But this does not mean that the muscles are equally powerful: in fact, the insect's flight muscle is much more powerful than the bird's or bat's. This is because the power of a gramme of muscle depends not only on the force that it generates per contraction, but also on how rapidly it can contract – in other words, how many contractions it can make per second. As we have seen, insect flight muscle is characterized by remarkably high contraction rates, and this is what makes it the most powerful muscle known in any animal. It is not difficult to understand how the power of a muscle relates to its contraction rate. If each contraction of an insect's flight muscles drive the wings through a single cycle, then the faster the muscles contract, the more rapid the wing beat, and the greater the aerodynamic force that is produced.

In order to continue working at these very high rates the flight muscles must have a guaranteed supply of fuel and oxygen. If the supply stopped for more than a moment the muscles would flag, in just the same way that the power of a car engine would fizzle out if you blocked its carburettor. The 'carburettor' of birds and bats is the bloodstream, delivering food and oxygen directly to the muscle cells via the infinitely ramifying capillaries. The bloodstream also supplies fuel to the flight muscles of insects – though not the oxygen, as we shall see in a moment.

Fuel comes in two forms, fat and carbohydrate, although these are processed in different ways and not all insects can use them to the same extent. Carbohydrate is obtained from the diet and can be stored in the body as sugar in the bloodstream and as glycogen in the muscles. Some insects, including the Diptera or true flies and the Hymenoptera (bees, wasps, saw-flies and ants), fuel the muscles exclusively with carbohydrate. Carbohydrate stores are usually limited in quantity although bees, for example, may carry additional stores of sugar in the honey stomach. Most insects that are wholly reliant on carbohydrates have little option but to feed regularly, if they are to keep flying.

The sources of carbohydrate are as varied as the diet itself. The richest sources are nectar and plant juices, since these contain high concentrations of sugars that require little digestion. Animal tissues and blood provide the necessary carbohydrates for predatory and blood-sucking insects, although the sugars from these sources can only be extracted after more prolonged digestion in the gut.

17. Two consecutive stages in the upward wing beat of the giant cuckoo wasp *Scolia flavifrons*. **A** shows the end of the downstroke; the fore wing is beginning to supinate in preparation for the upstroke. In **B** both wing pairs are moving backwards in the supinated position. The supinated wings are approaching the top of the upstroke; the leading edges of the opposite pairs are coming together in advance of the trailing edges.

18. Wing supination in the saw-fly *Tenthredo*. In **A,** the wings have just started the upstroke; the fore wing has supinated but the hind wing is still pronated. In **B,** the wings have completed the upstroke and are beginning the downstroke.

A

B

C

19. Four consecutive stages in the upstroke phase of the wing beat of the spider-hunting wasp *Sceliphron destillatorium*. In **A,** the wings are just beginning the upstroke. Note how the leading edges of the fore wings are being bent dowwards under pressure as they rise and begin to supinate. In **B,** fore and hind wings have both completely supinated and are moving backwards in the upside-down position, generating positive lift on their upper surfaces. In **C,** the wings have just reached the top of the stroke. And in **D,** the wings have separated and are beginning to move downwards although the trailing edges of the hind wings are still in contact.

D ▶

A

20. Three consecutive stages in the wing beat cycle of the digger wasp *Sphex*. **A** shows the start of the downstroke; the fore wing has pronated but the hind wing is still supinated. In **B,** both fore and hind wings are pronated and have nearly reached the end of the downstroke. **C** shows the start of the upstroke; fore and hind wings have both supinated and are developing lift on their upper surfaces as they move backwards.

A

21. The relationships between pronation and supination of the wings during the up-to-down stroke transition can be clearly seen in these rear views of a flying cicada *Tibicina haematodes*. In **A** the wings are ascending towards the top of the upstroke. The fore wing is clearly leading the hind, and the leading edges of both wings are in the 'nose-up' or supinated position. In **B,** the wings are beginning their descent and have twisted around their axes into the 'nose-down' or pronated position.

Not surprisingly, those insects that depend on regular supplies of dietary carbohydrate are also the most vulnerable to prolonged periods of food deprivation such as those that occur during migration. A locust flying continuously without feeding would exhaust all its carbohydrate reserves within about two hours. After this it has to call upon additional reserves from the fat stores. In this respect it is no different from a human marathon runner.

Fat can generally be stored in much greater quantities than carbohydrate, and it has two distinct advantages over carbohydrate as a source of energy for endurance activity. Each gramme of fat burned by the muscles yields twice as much energy as a gramme of carbohydrate, but the combustion of fat also yields more water as a by-product. This 'metabolic' water can be especially beneficial to insects migrating over large distances without access to water supplies.

For similar reasons, birds migrating from the southern Sahara across the desert to the North African seaboard are able to survive without drinking because they fuel their muscles on stored fat. The migration routes of these birds include oases but these are visited mainly to replenish food stocks, and drinking may not occur. The diet does not have to include fats as such since these can be readily synthesized in the bird's body from dietary carbohydrate. And so long as the fat stores are maintained, they continue to supply both the energy and water required to complete the journey.

Fuel, whether it is in the form of fat or carbohydrate, can only be consumed by the working muscles if there is an equally efficient delivery of oxygen from the environment to the muscle cells. As soon as an insect starts to fly, its need for oxygen shoots up enormously. The statistics on this subject are astounding: in some cases the demand increases four hundredfold compared to rest! The way delivery is achieved is completely different from that seen in birds or bats.

Instead of using its blood circulation, the insect delivers a stream of air directly from the atmosphere to the muscle cells via a system of ducts or tracheae which open into the body from a series of tiny pores or spiracles on the surface of the cuticle. In certain regions the tracheae dilate to form balloon-like air sacs which can function as bellows to pump the air through the duct system. The bellows are driven by rhythmical telescoping movements of the abdomen. These breathing movements can easily be seen in the abdomen of a bee as it rests to draw breath, as it were, between visits to flowers.

In some insects the spiracles are equipped with one-way valves which preserve a one-way flow of air through the tracheal system. Each time the air sacs dilate, the spiracles nearer the front end of the body open, allowing fresh air to be drawn in, whilst the spiracles nearer the tail end stay shut. Next, when the air sacs are compressed, the rear spiracles open, whilst those at the front close. As a result a stream of fresh air passes from the air sacs to the muscles, but at the same time the stale air from the muscles is driven out through the adbominal spiracles.

22. The bush-cricket *Decticus albifrons* is a very powerful leaper but it also extends its leap by beating its wings. Many insects begin their flight by leaping into the air. This primes the airflow around the wings and allows them to generate lift.

· 3 ·

INTO FLIGHT

The origin of flight in animals is one of the oldest chestnuts in the history of zoology. Reputations have been gained and lost in disputes over this subject, but the answer still remains shrouded in the mists of time and the fossil record. We may never know the exact circumstances that led the ancestors of modern birds, bats and insects to sacrifice the certainties of *terra firma* for an adventure in the air. I, for one, am not

dismayed: the subject would never again be quite so fascinating once the facts were fully unveiled.

One or two assumptions can be made with reasonable conviction. For instance, the three living groups of animals capable of flapping flight – birds, bats and insects – are all so remotely related on the evolutionary tree that they must have acquired the ability to fly independently of one another. It also seems reasonable to assume that the ability to glide would precede the evolution of true flapping flight, since gliding is a relatively simple form of locomotion requiring less structural specialization. Modern flying foxes and lemurs glide using flaps of skin stretched between the fore and hind limbs, a design also seen in the webbed fingers of a bat's wing. Indeed, the web of a bat's wing also stretches beyond its outer finger to its hind feet. The wings of extinct pterodactyls were constructed along similar lines, and the space in front of the elbow joint of a bird's wing is also spanned by a web of skin stretching from the upper arm to the wrist, the so-called patagium. Skin flaps, however, form only a tiny fraction of the lifting surface of a bird's wing compared to the primary and secondary flight feathers.

There is strong circumstantial evidence that the prototype flying insects also experimented with gliding, using shelf-like outgrowths from the thoracic segments to serve as fixed wings. Some fossil insects bear such extensions on all three segments, raising the possibility that they had a total of three pairs of wings although it seems unlikely that the first pair ever acquired the ability to flap. No remnant of this first pair of wings has survived in modern insects.

As far as birds are concerned, an alternative school of thought exists amongst scientists which argues that flight evolved in tandem with the ability to leap from the ground into the air. This hypothesis is interesting because it switches the emphasis away from the 'wings' to the legs. It has the added attraction that it coincides with the way most present-day birds launch themselves into the air. Wings can only begin to generate lift once a flow of air has been established across their surfaces. The priming current of air can be produced by launching 'passively' from an elevation such as a tree, in the same way that a 'hang-glider' gains lift by launching from the edge of a cliff. Alternatively, the animal can achieve the same result by leaping into the air.

In fact, leaping is not absolutely essential if the animal can make its wings beat fast enough from the start: swifts, swallows and flycatchers, for example, have very short legs, and are probably incapable of leaping but still manage to get airborne from a standing start. But these are exceptional. In contrast bats have very definitely opted for the passive 'no-legs' launch technique: by simply dropping into the air from their roost, they automatically create the necessary air currents across their wings.

This digression into the evolutionary origins of flight is not intended to muddy even further the waters of this lively debate, but it focuses our attention on the importance of take-off in a flying animal. Take-off is the most critical part of flight, because within those first few moments the conditions must be created that allow the wings to begin to work effectively. A lot of things must happen at the same time, and insects often get the sequence wrong. You have only to watch a beetle trying to take off from a grass stem; unless it has a firm foothold it will fall back, wings whirring ineffectively because the starting position was askew. The preliminaries to flight are quite complicated. For example, the insect will often perform a curious shuffling dance as though uncertain of the direction in which to take off. What it is doing is sensing the local air currents and orientating its body with respect to the direction of the sun. It is also trying to place its feet correctly beneath its centre of gravity in order to achieve maximum 'push-off' from the ground.

Leaping insects

Like birds, insects will usually launch into the wind, using the air movement to obtain a free injection of lift on the wings. This can easily be seen in grasshoppers such as *Oedipoda germanica* and *O. caerulescens*, which 'flash' their coloured wings as they leap away from an approaching observer. Almost invariably they take off straight into the wind, no matter how blustery it is, and even if it means flying for a moment into the face of the observer.

Just before the instant of launching, an insect will often be seen to 'rock back on its heels', fully flexing the backwardly directed 'knee' joint between the femur and tibia of the hind legs so that maximum extension can be gained at take-off. The same 'rocking back' movement can be seen in jackdaws, crows and herons preparing for flight, and you may have noticed a similar momentary crouching in songbirds such as blackbirds, thrushes, finches and larks at the moment before take-off. What these birds are doing is really no different from what a chicken does before leaping up on to its perch: flexing the prominent 'ankle' joint and in the process stretching the Achilles tendons that pass behind the heel. The elastic energy stored in the tendons then helps to catapult the body into the air during take-off.

In insects, we tend to associate leaping with particularly specialized groups such as fleas, grasshoppers, crickets, frog-hoppers and flea-beetles but many species of Hymenoptera (bees, wasps, saw-flies), Coleoptera (beetles) and true bugs (Hemiptera) have elongated hind legs which they use to leap into flight. In fact it is surprising how widespread the habit of leaping is. It crops up in some of the most unexpected situations, as a recent incident demonstrated to me.

The summer of 1989 in Great Britain, as in several recent years, was unusually hot and dry and came on the heels of a drought that had already begun to show its effects by early springtime. One day my good neighbour, septuagenarian Owen Walker, invited me to witness a curious event that he said was taking place in his garden pond. Among the occupants of this local haven of wildlife were numerous water boatmen of the species *Notonecta maculata*. This insect, along with its relative, *N. glauca*, is often referred to as a backswimmer on account of the fact that it swims in an upside-down position. The pond was now rapidly drying out and the boatmen, having decided that it was time to leave, were aligning themselves on the mud at the edge of the pond before launching into flight with an audible buzzing of their wings.

It was not the fact that the boatmen were flying that intrigued me; after all, flight is the normal way in which pond insects disperse their populations. What interested me more was the manner in which the insects took off.

On the face of it a water boatman is very badly designed for take-off. The hind legs, although very long and powerful, are specialized as oars sticking out straight from the side of the body, and it is difficult to see how they could be folded under the body to provide the necessary upward leverage for take-off. High-speed photography provided some interesting clues.

The preparations for take-off are fairly time-consuming, and it is difficult to provoke these insects into flight unless they are ready. To begin with, the boatman will need to dry out its wings and body. The fore wings are thickened and toughened, like the wing cases of beetles, and provide enclosure and protection for the membranous hind wings. In the closed condition, the fore wings overlap one another along the line of the 'keel' of the boatman's body: remember that the backswimmer swims upside-down and the 'keel' along its back actually faces downwards under water. With a tiny movement of its body, the insect 'unzips' the keel just enough to allow the air to permeate inside and dry out the hind wings.

When the boatman is ready for flight it then draws up its hind legs 'akimbo' so that the 'knee' formed by the femoro-tibial joint is pointing forwards and to the side, rather like the knees of a frog or a squatting sumo wrestler. This is quite different from the position of the 'knees' of a grasshopper, which point backwards and upwards. Nevertheless it seems to be effective, for the boatman suddenly extends the legs and hurls itself into the air (see photograph 4, page 17). Enough propulsion is gained by this movement to enable the boatman to become airborne, but high-speed photography showed that the insect was careful not to begin opening its wings until it was clear of the ground by at least one or two body lengths.

The photographs of the leaping water boatman showed that, despite all its specializations for an aquatic existence, it has managed to conserve the primal powers of leaping shown by its ancestors. After all, leaf-hoppers, frog-hoppers and tropical lantern flies are closely related to water boatmen, and all are expert leapers.

 A

 B

23. Leaping Homopteran bugs such as the frog-hoppers *Cercopis vulnerata* (**A**) and *Lepyromia* (**B**) probably have the highest take-off velocities, compared to their body size, of all jumping insects. High take-off velocities are associated with a streamlined body profile, but there must also be an elastic 'spring' somewhere in the hind legs. As the photographs show, the hind legs of frog-hoppers are not very long and the amount of muscle present in the thighs cannot be sufficient to account for the observed jump velocities. *Cercopis* regularly extends its wings at the instant of take-off, although it is not known to what extent breaking up the streamlined profile in this manner affects its speed of movement through the air.

This realization triggered off a train of thought in my mind about the broader problem faced by all insects during take-off, that of correctly timing the movements of the legs and wings. Having spent so many hours watching a tiny creature bob up and down in the air it came as something of a comfort that one might be able to expand from the particular to the universal! Consider the case of the water boatman itself. Why does it delay opening its wings at take-off? Wouldn't it make more sense simply to get the wings going at once, or even before take-off? Or is the delay intended to protect the wings from possible damage from brushing against the ground? Or is it part of a more complicated strategy to make the most effective use of the combined forces available from the legs and wings?

It could be argued, for instance, that if the wings were opened just before take-off they would destroy the smooth, streamlined profile of the body, increasing its drag and slowing down its movement through the air. On the other hand, when the water boatman delays opening its wings at take-off there is a risk that the initial momentum of the body will be lost, and with it the opportunity to make use of the priming airflow across the wings. During this critical period, every

millisecond counts. Opening the wings a fraction of a second too early or too late can make the difference between a successful launch and an untidy or unsuccessful launch. Of course, the boatman does not have to ponder this extremely complex equation every time it takes to flight! The species has had millions of years to experiment with it, and one must assume that by now it has got it just about right.

But the water boatman's solution may not be the same as that arrived at by other species faced with a similar problem. Different groups appear to have developed different strategies. Frog-hoppers, for instance, behave like *Notonecta* and wait until they have become airborne before opening their wings. In this way they make full use of their bullet-like profile to slide through the air and gain maximum speed during the first moments of take-off.

Yet not even all frog-hoppers can agree between themselves. Photograph 23A shows a species *Cercopis vulnerata* that begins to open its wings before it has left the ground. This insect proved to be a particularly interesting case because it showed how erroneous first impressions can be. I had been puzzling over the insect for months before I pointed a camera at it, and could have sworn that it never opened its wings until about a second after take-off, by which time it would be half a metre at least away from the point from which it had leaped. What my eyes saw was an insect with closed wing cases that suddenly leaped into the air, became virtually invisible for a half a second, then reappeared as something that was now flying with audibly buzzing wings. The reality that the high-speed camera saw was quite different, but I had to invent a super-fast high-speed shutter before I could solve the problem, as will be explained later in Chapter 9.

Launch problems in beetles

Beetles, when they are taking off, generally wait until their wings are completely extended before thrusting against the ground with their hind legs. The reasons for making sure the wings are open before take-off are again quite complex.

First, most beetles are not particularly well endowed for jumping anyway (leaving aside for the moment the specialized jumping beetles) and it makes sense for them to synchronize the extension of the legs with the first power stroke of the wings in order to pool the resources available in both sets of muscles. But even more important than this, actually opening the wings of a beetle is, in relative terms, an extraordinarily long and tedious process. The wing cases are often latched on to one another, and to the sides of the thorax, by an elaborate system of tiny bosses and sockets; disengaging these takes time. Once this is done, the membranous hind wings must then be extended, having previously been stowed away in a sometimes incredibly complex series of folds. The hind wing of the rove-beetle *Staphylinus olens*, the 'Devil's Coach Horse', contains at least a dozen such folds! The whole process may take half a second or more and, although this may not seem a long time to us, it is an eternity to a tiny insect. It also completely rules out any possibility of the kind of millisecond timing between legs and wings achieved by the water boatman.

As we saw earlier, beetles are remarkably accident-prone when it comes to take-off, and examples of gross mistimings of the legs and wings are commonplace. Apart from being quite amusing to watch, these miscalculations give a graphic demonstration of the problem from the beetle's point of view.

One sees the beetle going through all the usual motions, fastidiously gathering its feet beneath the centre of gravity of its body, tiptoeing on its four front feet in order to align the axis of the body with the projected angle of take-off, and finally straining to open the elytra and release the membranous hind wings. The whole sequence of events appears to be strictly programmed and once it has begun the beetle seems compelled to follow it through rigidly to completion, even though hitches may arise on the way. Often the insect will reach the final stage of the sequence when for one reason or another the elytra fail to open. But it is too late. Driven by its instincts, the insect leaps feebly into the air – only to tumble back ignominiously to the ground.

Flight-assisted leaping in mantids

Not all insects get quite so flustered at take-off as beetles. Mantids, for example, are far more deliberate in their preparations. It may come as a surprise to some readers that mantids can fly at all since we tend to think of them as secretive denizens of bushes and grassland, relying on stealth and cryptic or camouflage coloration to capture their prey and avoid detection by predators. Indeed many species only fly when hard pressed, but when they do they reveal wings that billow and glint in the sunshine and their lace-like beauty makes you gasp. Other species, such as the *Iris oratoria* shown in photograph 44 on page 86–7, fly much more readily and will often be attracted to lighted rooms at night.

The flight of mantids, although quite powerful, is short-lived and it is probably best to regard flying in many of these insects as an instrument of last resort when other behavioural measures have failed to deter an aggressor. Depending on the level of threat, mantids will show a range of behavioural responses. 'Rigour' is a straightforward cryptic response in which the insect contrives to resemble an inert piece of vegetation. The huge raptorial 'arms' become drawn tight in alongside the long 'neck', immobilizing the whole of the front end of the body into a stick-like appendage. If this simple device fails, some species resort to making scraping noises with the stiff, papery fore wings, or flicking open the hind wings to reveal distracting patterns of 'flash coloration'.

The easiest response of all is to scuttle deeper and deeper into the vegetation in the hope that the aggressor will not be drawn into pursuit. This solution is simple but effective, as I have often learnt to my cost when endeavouring to capture specimens of the praying mantis *Mantis religiosa* in southern Spain. Females of the Santa Teresa, as it is locally known, can measure up to 8–9 cm in length. They are common in fields and roadside verges, though you might never know it because they merge in so well with the vegetation.

The Santa Teresa often chooses to secrete itself within the branches of one of the most off-putting plants to be found in Mediterranean Europe: *Calicotome*, the spiny broom. *Calicotome* ranks alongside the spiny acacia *Acacia karoo*, the jujube bush *Zisyphus* and the prickly-pear cactus *Opuntia* as a cheap and natural substitute for barbed wire, and not surprisingly all four shrubs are used for this purpose by farmers in Mediterranean Europe and North Africa. When a mantis begins to withdraw stubbornly into the recesses of its lair, it renders itself practically inextricable. The spines of *Calicotome* are several centimetres long, and the consequences of over-zealous pursuit of a retreating mantis can be painful. I have personally found that the Santa Teresa almost invariably wins this uneven contest, but on the rare occasions that I have succeeded in flushing out an individual the reasons for its stubbornness become quickly apparent. For when it attempts to fly, its body, which has become gorged throughout the spring and summer months on a plentiful supply of grasshoppers, pitches heavily backwards, stalls the wings and abruptly curtails its progress. Removed from its natural environment it presents a relatively easy target for any predator large enough to tackle it, such as a hawk, shrike or snake.

Mantids fortunately turn out to be a good choice of subject for studying the different timing strategies that can be used in controlling the leg and wing movements during take-off. Some species have already begun to open their wings by the time their feet have left the ground, while others wait until their body is well clear of the ground. Of course there are occasions when the insect may choose not to use its wings at all. It would be wrong to think that individuals are rigidly tied to a single strategy; within limits they can vary the strategy to suit the occasion. For instance, faced with an imminent threat, such as a bird that has suddenly landed within centimetres of its body, the most expedient strategy for the mantis is simply to leap out of the way at once without bothering to open its wings. This may result in a much shorter leap, but it gains time for the insect.

One of the most interesting examples of timing strategy is provided by the diminutive mantid *Ameles spallanziana*, another species found commonly around the Mediterranean. *Ameles* may be rather drab in appearance, but it is an expert at coordinating its many appendages. It was purely by chance that I noticed something unusual about the launch technique used by *Ameles*.

With this particular mantid it is never a question of leaping unknowingly into the dark. It will survey the exact spot towards which it will leap by swivelling its head slowly and repeatedly from side to side as though fixing the coordinates of the image first with one eye, then with the other. Very possibly the insect is employing the method of 'parallax' to compute the distance of the spot, just as in the case of the human eye. This method relies on the fact that each eye sees the object from a slightly different angle and the brain uses these slight discrepancies in image alignment to estimate the distance. In *Ameles* this purpose is well served by the fact that its eyes are rather widely spaced on its head.

A

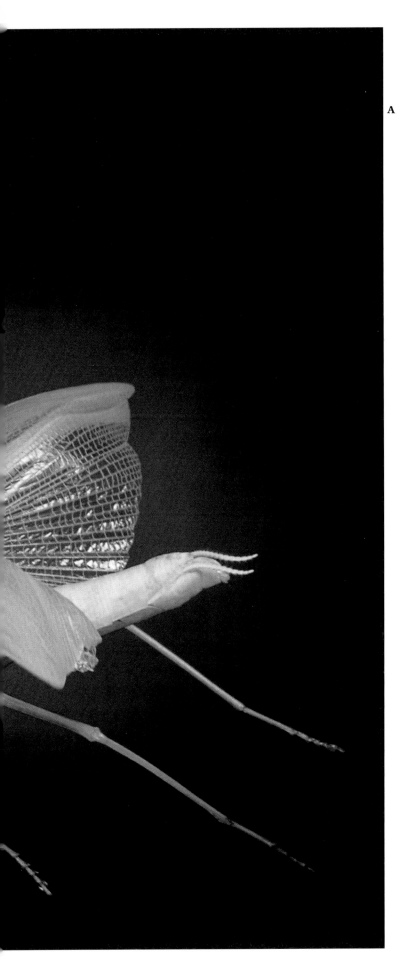

24. These two photographs of a praying mantis *Mantis religiosa* leaping into flight show the sequence of opening of the fore and hind wings. The pleated membranous hind wings are folded concertina-wise beneath the leathery fore wings. In **A** the fore wings are beginning to move forward, allowing the hind wing to be 'drawn out' into its expanded form. In **B** both wing pairs are fully opened and about to undergo the first downstroke.

B

A

The most interesting thing occurs next, although it is almost impossible to discern the exact details with the naked eye. Watching the insect on several occasions I had the impression that, just before it leaped, it momentarily hesitated, flicked open its wings into a raised position, and only then kicked out against the ground. High-speed photography confirmed what the naked eye could only guess at. During the very brief moment of hesitation, the wings are brought straight up from their resting position to their full height above the body. For a few milliseconds they hang poised there, the two wings of each side placed back-to-back with their neighbours. Next, in one and the same moment, the wings are driven down and the hind legs kicked out from behind, so that power is delivered simultaneously from both sets of appendages.

Ameles seems to have come up with the ideal timing strategy, but that momentary delay before take-off, however brief, does introduce a risk. A moment may be all that is needed for a predator to make a successful strike. *Ameles*, like the water boatman earlier, is faced with a dilemma: when threatened, it must weigh the imminence of the threat against the time that will be gained or lost by employing the wings and legs together or separately. Just as in the case of the water boatman, milliseconds count for a great deal.

This may seem a little dramatic as we contemplate, from the ease of our suburban garden chairs, the contented drone of bees, the unhurried dancing of butterflies and the random, heat-crazed hopping of grass-hoppers that appear to have nothing better to do. But if we really want to gain an accurate

25. Sexual dimorphism, in which the male and the female of the species differ markedly in appearance, is common amongst mantids and may have far-reaching effects on locomotory performance, as in the mantid *Ameles spallanziana*. The male *Ameles* (**A**) is much more slender than the female and is fully winged although, as in this case, the wings may not always be recruited during leaping. The female (**B**) is much more stoutly built and has short, non-functional wings. The heavy abdomen of this female has pitched her head-over-heels through the air, although her eyes and prehensile fore legs remain firmly focused on the point at which she will land.

B

picture of the forces that have moulded the split-second behaviour of the ancestors of these insects, we must visit the tropical rainforests. There we will find the environmental pressure cookers in which the war of natural selection is continuously being waged between predator and prey, pitting the cunning of one against the alertness of the other. Experiments in the split-second timing of behaviour are being carried out in millions of species, during every second of the day. To say, in these circumstances, that 'milliseconds count' is probably a gross understatement.

A specific example might help to make the point clearer. Not long ago a colleague recounted one particularly interesting aspect of work that he had been doing in the Brazilian rainforest. It involved the feeding behaviour of a particular group of Amazonian monkeys called Talapoins.

These miniature primates weigh only 200 g or so, and can make a substantial meal out of a medium-sized bush-cricket, praying mantid or beetle living within and beneath the forest canopy. To avoid capture, the prey needs to be agile and alert, since the monkeys comb very carefully through each item of foliage using their nimble fingers. In addition, some monkeys organize themselves into groups of 'beaters' whose job it is to flush out the prey, and 'collectors' who wait below to catch it as it falls.

But this is really only the beginning of the insect's plight. From dawn until dusk, and then all through the tropical night, a steady succession of creatures emerges, each one determined to take its share of the same food supply. When the insects are not being hounded by birds, chameleons and lizards during the day, they are hiding from snakes and insectivorous mammals during the hours of darkness. It is this endless chain of predator–prey encounters that hones to perfection the split-second reactions referred to above.

Leaping and escape from predators
In a rather roundabout way, this digression into the biology of mantids and monkeys helps us to understand how perfect syn-

chronization of wing and leg can be so important to a leaping insect such as *Ameles*. But it would be misleading to think that the only reason a leaping insect uses its wings is to gain extra power. Perhaps even more importantly, recruiting the wings enables the jumping insect to exercise a measure of control over its trajectory that would otherwise be impossible.

When an insect jumps without using its wings, its speed, direction and length of stay in the air are all absolutely determined the moment its feet leave the ground. From that point it has no further control over its future until it hits the ground again. But, as we saw in Chapter 1, being able to sow confusion into the mind of an aggressor by using the wings continuously to vary the escape path may actually be more valuable than trying to outstrip him. Again, a few examples will serve to illustrate the point.

The wart-biter *Decticus verrucivorus* is a very large bush-cricket which inhabits mountainous areas of Europe. Although equipped with very powerful hind legs, *Decticus* is a plodding kind of insect; its principal shortcoming is that, when pursued, it tends to leap rather predictably in a straight line, like a frog. It has very large wings but never seems to use them. These characteristics make *Decticus* a very easy target, at least to a pursuing naturalist!

Take now another bush-cricket, the beautiful but odd-looking *Acrida hungarica* shown in photograph 26. *Acrida* has slender thighs so that, although it can leap, only limited power is available in the legs. But if the air temperature is high enough a disturbed *Acrida* will spread its wings and fly, if only for a few metres. And it will vary its flight path. To the extent that *Acrida* proves a more difficult insect to capture than *Decticus*, the strategy seems to work.

In *Acrida* we see the rudiments of an in-flight avoidance strategy that is developed to a much more telling effect in a group of grasshoppers known collectively for their ability to display 'flash coloration'. Familiar European examples are *Oedipoda caerulescens* and *Psophus caeruleus*, both of which carry very distinctive colour patterns

26. *Acrida* is an example of a bush-cricket with very slender thighs containing relatively little muscle. What it lacks in springing power it makes up for in its ability to make brief bursts of weak but erratic flight.

on the hind wings. As these insects leap they simultaneously break out into a random zig-zag flight, 'flashing' the wing colours to distract any potential predator. It is virtually impossible to follow their flight path, and the whole effect is compounded by the fact that the body and front wings are cryptically coloured so that when the insect finally alights it simply dissolves into the background. The only predictable elements in the escape flight of these insects, as seen earlier in this chapter, is that they will always take off into the wind.

A final example will suffice. The Egyptian grasshopper *Anacridium aegyptium* combines the 'crazy flight' behaviour of *Oedipoda* and *Psophus* with the artfulness of the Santa Teresa of southern Spain. The Egyptian grasshopper is a very large insect that relishes the arid, stony steppes of North Africa and parts of Mediterranean Europe. It survives in this hostile environment very largely on account of the shelter that it receives from the jujube bush *Zisyphus*, otherwise known as the Crown of Thorns.

In some inexplicable manner, *Zisyphus* still manages to draw moisture from parched soils above which shade temperatures for much of the year hover around 40–45 degrees centigrade, and even birds refuse to fly between dawn and dusk. The chief enemy of many insects in North Africa, indeed the chief enemy of much of the native fauna and flora of all the wilder upland parts of the Mediterranean countries, is goats – not because they eat insects, but because they eat almost every plant in sight. Fortunately, even their tongues find the Crown of Thorns totally repellent and so the Egyptian grasshopper has a safe sanctuary.

Like many of the 'brushwood' plants of stony steppe and desert, *Zisyphus* tends to grow in fairly evenly scattered clumps rather than in large swathes, and the flight behaviour of the Egyptian grasshopper is perfectly matched to this environment. When flushed out of a bush it pursues a random, zig-zag flight path which will confuse an enemy but also pitch it down close to a neighbouring bush, avoiding too much exposure to open ground in between. As in the case of *Oedipoda* and *Psophus*, these bursts of flight last at most a few seconds, and it is difficult to know for certain whether any real control is exercised over the flight path or whether the insects are simply programmed to behave as randomly as possible, like rapidly deflating balloons careering madly around in the air.

Leaping with the aid of springs

So far we have looked at some of the ways in which leaping forms part of the normal lifestyle of an insect, whether as a natural prelude to flight or as an integral component in a complex behavioural response. At this behavioural level, the facts all seem to tie in very satisfactorily. It is when we examine more closely some of the physical attributes of the legs and their muscles that a kind of physiological paradox seems to emerge.

For instance, the velocity of a leaping insect just as it leaves the ground is often found to be many times greater than the maximum speed at which the leg muscles can possibly contract, even after taking into account the levering action occurring in the various leg joints. In fact, the acceleration time – the time during which the legs are extending just before take-off – is often astonishingly small. It is less than a thousandth of a second, for instance, in a jumping flea. A muscle could not possibly contract within this brief period of time. How are we to explain this contradiction?

To put the problem into perspective, let us consider another related problem, but one much nearer to home. Why is it not possible for a man to throw a stone with his hand as far as he can shoot the same stone with a catapult? After all, in both cases he is using the same power available in his arms, and it is not as though a small stone is a heavy object. The difference is that the man throwing the stone, no matter how hard he strives, cannot possibly move his arm through the air fast enough, because his muscles have only a limited speed of contraction. This has nothing to do with the missile he is throwing: it is a limitation in the arm itself. The catapult is an instrument designed by our war-like ancestors to overcome this limitation. The catapult acts as a spring that stores all the energy put into it as the arm is slowly drawn back. Then all of this accumulated energy is released explosively, making the stone shoot through the air at high velocity.

27. The immature or nymphal stages of grasshoppers and bush-crickets look like miniature adults except that they lack fully formed wings. They are all competent 'hoppers' but lack the ability of many of the adults to extend the leap by using the wings. **A:** migratory locust *Locusta migratoria.* **B:** dark bush-cricket *Pholidoptera griseoaptera.* **C:** Egyptian grasshopper *Anacridium aegyptium.*

C

A

28. Bush-crickets (family Tettigoniidae) have longer, slimmer hind legs than grasshoppers (family Acrididae) and the muscle is concentrated near the top of the femur, thereby cutting down the pendular moment of the legs. It seems unlikely that the 'knee' joint between the femur and tibia is thick enough to accommodate an elastic 'spring' similar to that found in grasshopper legs, but the increased length of the legs compensates for this deficiency. All three species shown here are short-winged or brachypterous, and the wings are used exclusively as sound-producing organs. **A:** speckled bush-cricket *Leptophyes punctatissima*. **B:** dark bush-cricket *Pholidoptera grisecaptera*. **C:** *Rhacocleis* sp.

B

C

A similar thing happens in the case of many jumping insects. They overcome the physiological deficiencies in their leg muscles by cranking up a spring that is then held ready to be released at high speed at the appropriate moment. They can thus catapult their bodies into the air at far greater speeds than could ever be achieved by muscle contraction. The principle is ingenious, and the hardware to make it work involves remarkable innovations of design.

To meet the task of energy storage, insects have developed specialized rubber-like proteins. In fleas, for example, the spring consists of a pad of rubber-like protein at the base of the hind legs. When the legs are drawn in towards the body they squeeze the rubber pad. Grasshoppers and locusts store the elastic energy in a strip of stretchable cuticle located on the outside of the 'knee' joint of the hind leg, between the femur and tibia. Because it lies on the outer side of the joint, the strip becomes stretched when the joint is flexed. The joint is held in the flexed position by a 'catch'. When the insect wants to jump, the catch is released and the joint springs into the extended position. You can actually see grasshoppers and crickets 'cranking' their legs just before they take off. No matter how hard you press it, a grasshopper will only leap when it has managed to flex its knee joint fully, stretch the elastic strip and momentarily engage the catch. There is no question of making 'half a leap' with only half-flexed knees.

Launching by free-fall

Although leaping is one of the most obvious ways that insects can launch into flight, common sense tells us that there must be other ways too. A glance at the flimsy legs of a cranefly, lacewing or butterfly hardly suggests that these insects possess the necessary strength to leap into the air. Some insects must have evolved special ways of generating lift with their wings from a standing start. Others have opted for the method used by bats, which procure the necessary priming airflow around the wings by simply dropping into the air as they take off.

29. The bush-cricket *Decticus albifrons* has very large functional wings that can sustain powerful flight for a few seconds to extend the range of its leap. Depending on circumstances, the wings may (**A**) or may not (**B**) be used during leaping.

◀ **A**

B

30. Grasshoppers tend to have shorter legs than bush-crickets and thicker 'knees' that contain an elastic 'spring' increasing the power of the jump. Many species, such as the common field grasshopper *Chorthippus brunneus* (**A**), and the blue-winged grasshopper *Oedipoda caerulescens* (**B**), have fully functional wings which are sometimes used to assist leaping. Others, such as *Calliptamus* (**C**), are short-winged and do not have this choice available to them.

Some species of dragonflies and their relatives, the damselflies, experience great difficulty if they try to take off from level ground. In such circumstances it is obvious that their short legs are powerless to propel the body into the air, and all the wings can do is rattle noisily against the ground, unable to develop lift. But these insects are usually careful to avoid landing on the ground. I have seen other species of dragonfly launching from the ground, but on most of these occasions there was a moderately strong breeze to help lift-off. Normally a dragonfly coming into land will select a spot such as a piece of tall vegetation, which allows it to hang vertically at rest so that the next take-off can easily be achieved by falling backwards and downwards into the air.

The free-fall technique, as we might describe it, is also used by craneflies, lacewings, mayflies, ant-lions and many other insects which are commonly found hanging vertically from twigs and grass stems or clinging to the undersides of vegetation. Short-legged beetles, such as ladybirds and click-beetles, also make use of gravity to achieve lift-off. Before flight these insects will often crawl to the ends of pieces of vegetation and only then, when they are teetering on the edge of 'thin air', will they feel confident to open their wings and fly.

Sometimes casual observations, which appeared to have little significance at the time they were made, later turn out to provide the vital clue to a problem. Several years ago I spent many hours trying to photograph the process of 'gift presentation' that takes place between the male and female of a species of empid fly *Empis tessellata*. These are largish, predatory flies which hunt on the wing and are capable of overcoming a medium-sized cranefly without too much difficulty.

Once the prey has been seized, the male presents it to the female. Somehow during this encounter, which again takes place in the air, he contrives to grasp her around the body with the second and third pairs of his legs. Noticeably, however, he leaves the front pair of legs free. Whilst the female is engaged burying her proboscis into the unfortunate

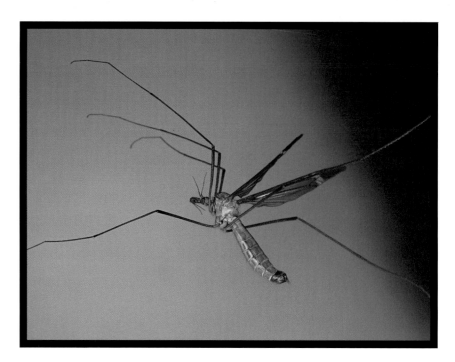

donation, her suitor takes the opportunity to copulate with her.

At the time I was specifically interested in the range of different kinds of prey that the male was seen to offer the female, but what became more interesting was the mechanical feats performed by the male, who was able to continue flying, carrying a load equivalent to at least twice his own body weight. Borne down by such a weight, he obviously cannot fly very far and cannot possibly take off from the ground. Even without any additional burdens, such as gifts for the female, mating insects are especially vulnerable from attack by predators, since their respective genitalia cannot be disengaged immediately and each partner obviously greatly hinders the movements of the other.

This is where the male empid's front legs come in useful. Once he has secured his mate, he immediately seeks out dense vegetation and suspends himself plus mate and prey from the underside of a leaf. Although this places enormous strain on his front legs, it affords the best conditions from which to launch into the next flight.

Empis tessellata is not an isolated case since most empids share the same habit of gift presentation and bearing away of the lucky female. Many other insects are also

31. It seems unlikely that the delicate legs of craneflies (family Tipulidae) such as the tipulid shown here can provide significant thrust to help take-off. The habit of suspending the body from vegetation at rest helps because it provides 'free-fall' lift at the start of flight.

32. Scorpion flies such as *Panorpa commonis* shown here inhabit dense foliage and are rather weak fliers. They often rest on the edges of leaves and this makes emergency take-off easier since they can gain lift quickly by tumbling into the air.

capable of flight *in coitus*, perhaps the best-known examples being dragonflies and damselflies. In these cases the female is free to beat her wings and contribute her share of support to the 'double payload'. The same division of labour occurs in mating craneflies, which are often seen flying in tandem in the breeding season. Mating butterflies, particularly whites, will readily take to flight – although in this case only one of the sexes, probably the female, does all the work.

Paired beetles will also attempt to fly if disturbed, but often with futile consequences – the male is usually mounted on the back of the female, clasping the sides of her wing cases and making it impossible for her to open them. In such circumstances female soldier beetles such as *Cantharis rustica* will feverishly strive to dislodge the male with their hind legs. She may succeed in dislodging him, but he continues to be attached by his genitalia and often 'freezes' into a pupa-like state. He is now content to allow himself to be hauled along by the distraught female like an unwanted piece of cargo.

Launch techniques in butterflies
Finally in this chapter we come to those insects, such as butterflies, that rely neither on leaping nor on gravitational assistance to launch into flight. And in many ways these are the most interesting.

Anyone who has stalked a butterfly feeding upon a flower will know that, although the insect appears to be engrossed in its task, it always has 'one eye on the look-out', so that if you approach just a little too closely it takes off like lightning. Often it goes straight up into the air. Rapid, vertical take-off is only one of the many remarkable characteristics of butterfly flight, as will be seen in Chapter 7. But for the present we shall concentrate on the mechanism behind the vertical take-off.

The clue can be found in the behaviour of the butterfly just before it takes off. You may have noticed that, although butterflies often browse with their wings spread in order to catch the sunlight, as soon as they sense any danger they will swiftly close their wings

above their body. This not only exposes the more cryptically coloured undersides of the wings, but also puts the wings into a state of readiness. In a few butterflies this is the normal posture and the upper wing surface is rarely seen at rest: insect photographers will be aware of the frustration of trying to snap the upper wing surface of a clouded yellow *Colias crocea*!

33. Three consecutive stages in the take-off manoeuvre of the clouded yellow butterfly *Colias crocea*. Immediately before take-off the wings are closed together above the body. **A** was taken at the end of the first downstroke, the wings having been pulled down vertically at high speed from their resting positions. The resultant pressure on the lower wing surfaces has begun to pitch the body backwards and upwards. Consequently the body axis has become aligned almost vertically in preparation for the first upstroke, which is just beginning to occur in **B**. The fore wing is already supinating ahead of the hind wing, and as it moves backwards in the horizontal plane it will generate lift on its upper surface. The hind wing will follow suit. In **C** both wings have clapped together at the end of the first upstroke and are now peeling apart at the start of the second downstroke.

C

34. Three consecutive stages (**A, B, C**) in the peeling of the wings during the downstroke of the woodland grayling butterfly *Hipparchia fagi*. The insect is viewed from behind and is flying away from the observer.

35. These paired views from above (**A**) and below (**B**) the body of a flying red admiral butterfly *Vanessa atalanta* illustrate the kite-like outline of the body at the very end of the peeling process, when only the inner margins of the hind wings remain in contact.

A

B ▶

The trick that the butterfly uses to achieve vertical take-off is to beat its wings straight down through their full height. This is why the wings are put on alert at the approach of danger. The wings start off with their tips in contact above the body and finish the stroke a few thousandths of a second later with the tips almost in contact just below the body. There is no attempt to slide the wings smoothly through the air at an angle, as was described in Chapter 1. They are simply made to beat the air face-on like a paddle. At least this is what the situation appears to be when seen from the position of an observer looking up at the underside of the insect.

But if we look closely from above the butterfly's body we see something else taking place. The wings of each side are not separating rigidly, like two plates, but are steadily peeling apart as they descend, like two pages of a book. The peeling starts from the leading edges of the front wings and progresses steadily back towards the trailing edges of the hind wings until the two sides have fully separated.

The result of this peeling process is that a vacuum forms between the separating wings; this simultaneously draws in a current of air from above and draws up the body of the insect from below. The process takes only a small fraction of a second, and in that time the body is suddenly sucked upwards into the air. The force on the body is in fact greater than this, since not only is it being sucked up from above but it is also being driven up from below by the pressure on the wings as they 'slap' the air beneath them.

The story does not end here. By the time the wings have completed their first downstroke the body is not only accelerating upwards but has also been pitched backwards. The purpose of the backward pitch is to align the body axis in preparation for the second half of the vertical take-off manoeuvre: the upstroke. As the upstroke starts the body is tilted almost vertically, making the wings travel horizontally with respect to the ground. Also the leading edge of the fore wing has been supinated nose-up so that the wings move backwards with their

A

upper surfaces facing downwards. Therefore throughout the upstroke, the wings continue to present a positive angle of attack to the air and produce a vertically directed lifting force sustaining the upward momentum received from the first downstroke.

Wing peeling is not confined to butterflies but is a specialized method of lift production seen in many insect groups (see photographs 36–40), although it is perhaps best suited for the take-off and climbing phases of flight. More details of this and other ways of generating lift will be discussed in Chapter 7.

36. Many groups of insects, including various true flies or Diptera, employ a 'clap and fling' or 'clap and peel' technique of wing movement to provide additional lift during take-off. Two consecutive stages of the wing beat cycle are illustrated in this psilid fly. A moment before **A** was taken the wings would have been 'clapped' together in the mid-line above the body, as shown in the photograph 11A. Now the leading edge has pronated and is moving downwards at the start of the stroke. The trailing edges have not yet pronated and are being drawn together to perform either a 'peel' or a 'near peel', depending on whether or not actual physical contact is made. In **B**, the wings have separated completely and both leading and trailing edges have pronated.

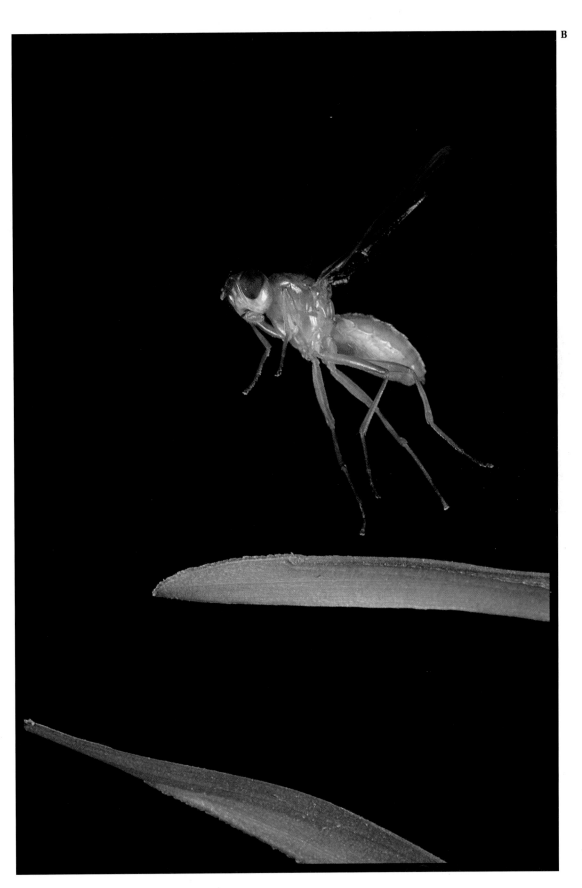

B

A   **B ▶**

37. The song of the male Italian cricket *Oecanthus pellucens* fills the night skies of Mediterranean Europe for much of the year. Such is its beauty that one observer commented: 'If the moon could sing, it would sound like this.' Sound is produced by rubbing together the highly modified fore wings, whose ribbed 'harp' can be seen in the photographs. *Oecanthus* is nocturnal, but is extremely reluctant to fly in the dark. However it will readily use its wings to assist leaping. These two photographs illustrate how *Oecanthus* cleverly synchronizes the extension of the hind legs with the first downstroke of the wings. The hind wings are steadily peeled apart during the stroke, and the progress of the peel is evident on looking from **A** to **B**. Peeling produces an energy boost in the wings by a specialized aerodynamic process.

A

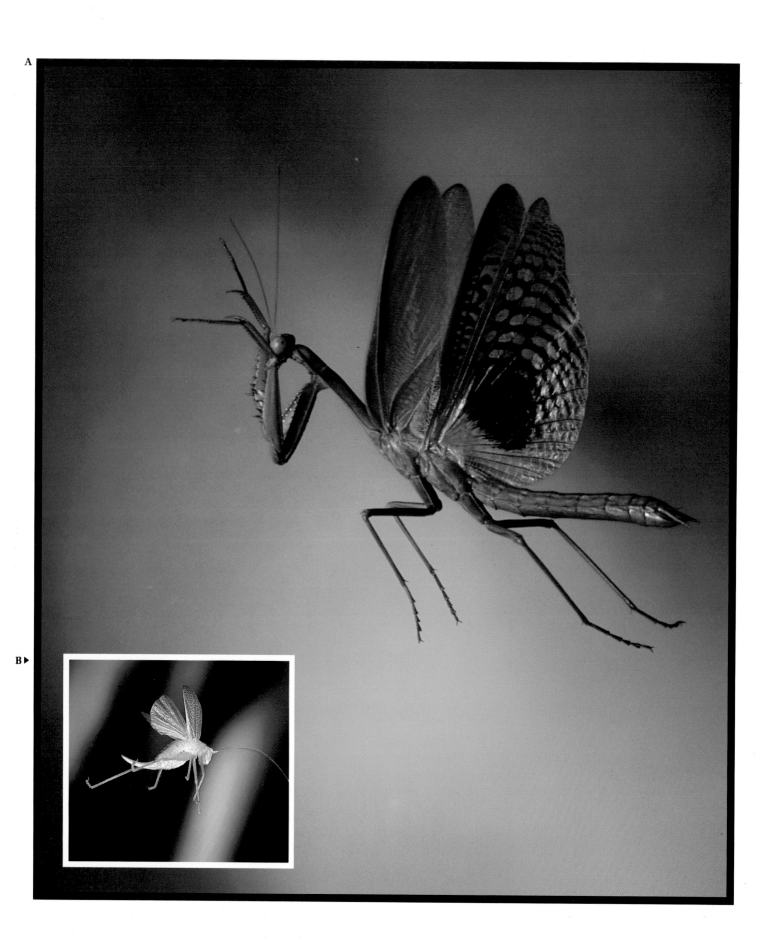

B ▶

38. The membranous hind wings of mantids, grasshoppers and crickets are ideally suited to the peeling process, which is a way of gaining extra lift particularly during take-off. Various stages of hind wing peel are seen in these photographs of (**A**) mantis *Iris oratoria*, (**B**) oak bush-cricket *Meconema thalassinum*, (**C**) great green bush-cricket *Tettigonia viridissima*.

A

B

C

39. The tiny flea-beetle *Phyllotreta* has enlarged hind femora adapted for jumping. Depending on circumstances, the wings may or may not be used to assist jumping. In **A** the wing cases remain unopened, whilst in **B** and **C** the wings have been used either to extend the leap or to give directional control whilst the insect is airborne. **B** and **C** are in sequence, and show how the hind wings peel apart during the downstroke. In **B** the hind wings are at their maximum height and have just pronated, swinging the trailing edges into contact. In **C** the wings have completely separated and are approaching the bottom of the stroke.

40. 'Clap and fling' is illustrated in these photographs of a digger wasp. In **A** the opposite wings are clapped together above the body. In **B** the leading edges of the fore wings have pronated and the wings are flinging apart with their trailing edges still in contact. **C** shows the wings proceeding downwards after separation.

◀ **A**

B

C

41. The praying mantis *Mantis religiosa* is a very heavy insect but is still capable of flight in an emergency. The delicate appearance of the wings belies their incredible strength which is based on flexibility and being able to deform under stress.

·4·

WING STRENGTH AND FLEXIBILITY

In Chapter 3 we saw how an insect's wing must possess not only strength but also flexibility. Most of the strength lies in the veins, but these too must be able to bend under stress – although not to the same degree as the membrane lying between the veins.

The greatest marvel of the insect wing is that it combines both of these qualities, strength and deformability, into an incredibly lightweight construction. The weight of most insects' wings can be measured not in grammes, but in millionths of a gramme. Indeed only the most sensitive of modern electronic balances would be capable of accurately weighing the wing of, say, a small fly. It is unlikely that any available balance could measure the weight of the wing of a tiny thrips or thunder-fly.

And there is good reason why the wing needs to be so light. It is far more important for an insect to keep down the weight of its wings than it is in the case of man-made aircraft, because the insects' wings must vibrate at up to several hundred times per second and in these circumstances its 'effective' weight, or inertia, increases enormously. Even an extremely light wing, therefore, imposes a considerable inertial load on the wing muscles when it is made to beat very rapidly.

Pleats and folds in wings

Most of this chapter will be concerned with the way the wing is designed to withstand the dynamic stresses imposed upon its fabric by its own weight and vibration. At the same time we should not overlook the obvious fact that for most of the insect's life the wings may be doing nothing at all, and it is therefore important to have ways of folding them out of harm's way. This requirement too will be reflected in the design of the wing. The designer of the sail of a boat faces a similar technical problem: its shape should not only enable it to catch the wind, but also allow it to be furled quickly and conveniently.

A few insects, including dragonflies, lack any wing-folding mechanism, and simply hold their wings outstretched at rest. In general, however, inability to fold the wings would severely restrict freedom of movement on the ground and insects have evolved a wide range of wing folding techniques to avoid this problem. These vary from simply closing the wings flat or roofwise over the abdomen, to the extremely elaborate methods used by beetles to crimp and tuck the wings beneath the elytra. The wings of many beetles are much longer than the abdomen or the elytra, and the fastidious process of folding them away after use is only made possible by the presence of numerous strategically arranged creases in the wing surface: the wing of a rove-beetle, for instance, may have a dozen or more such creases!

Wing folding is just one facet of a much more general phenomenon that we can see in the design of the body of insects: the use of strategic folding mechanisms to assist in movements of the various articulated sections of the head, thorax, abdomen and limbs. We shall see a fascinating example of this in Chapter 8, which deals with the mechanism of tail extension in springtails. The biomechanical and indeed the ergonomic implications of surface-folding techniques in joint-bodied animals like insects have hardly begun to be explored by biologists or engineers, but the widespread use of folding suggests that fundamental design principles must be at work.

You do not need to look far in the man-made world to find similar examples of strategic folding: the crease in a pair of pressed trousers, the method of furling and unfurling an umbrella, the foldaway deck-chair or the pleats in a woman's skirt. Perhaps the best example is a book: the arrangement of text into a series of foldaway pages represents an extraordinary technological advance over scroll writing. None of these designs came about by chance; they have evolved as the best solutions to tricky folding problems, sometimes after centuries of trial and error. There is no reason why similar design principles should not eventually be identified in insects' wings and bodies.

One of these principles must surely be the fact, already well known to engineers, that the introduction of a simple fold or pleat into a thin flexible membrane, like a sheet of paper or an insect's wing, can transform it into a structure possessing unexpected strength and resistance to bending. The point can be demonstrated quite easily by using a sheet of foolscap paper and a 500 g weight (see Figure 9). Whereas a flat sheet offers no resistance whatever to loads applied to its free edge or at right-angles to its surface, folding the paper into a pleated

Figure 9. A sheet of paper and a weight can be used to demonstrate the structural properties of pleating in a membrane. An unfolded sheet of paper has no resistance to compression and buckles easily when a force is applied to its edge (**A**) or at right-angles to its surface (**B**). If the paper is simply folded into a small number of pleats it gains the ability to bear weight like a column (**C**) or a horizontal beam (**D**). In the latter case, the bearing strength can be further increased by pinching the folds together at the base to form a fan (**E**).

42. This praying mantis *Mantis religiosa* (left) appears remarkably graceful as it leaps through the air. The sharply upturned end of the abdomen is noticeable and probably helps to shift the centre of gravity of the body forward, preventing backward pitching about the wing axis. The side view allows us to see the main veins and flexion lines in the wings, details of which are shown in Figure 10.

43. The hind wings of this mantid *Ameles spallanziana* (below) are in the middle of the downstroke, and the pressure on their lower surface has blown them out like an umbrella. During this process the pleats of the wing become flattened and the veins that strengthen the pleats are forced to bend downwards. The resultant umbrella-like camber produced on the wing increases its effectiveness as a lift-producing surface.

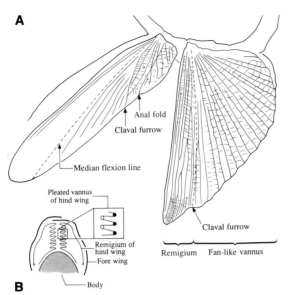

A

Anal fold
Claval furrow
Median flexion line
Pleated vannus of hind wing
Remigium of hind wing
Fore wing
Body
B
Claval furrow
Remigium   Fan-like vannus

Figure 10. Front and hind wings of the praying mantis *Mantis religiosa* (**A**), drawn from photograph 42. The wings are positioned near the lowest point of the stroke. Structurally, both wings are divided by the claval furrow into a leathery front part (the remigium) and a more membranous rear part (the clavus). In the hind wing the clavus is greatly expanded to form a highly pleated vane or vannus. In addition to the claval furrow, the fore wing has two more flexion lines: the median flexion line crossing the wing surface obliquely from base to tip, and the much smaller anal fold cutting obliquely across the clavus. **B** shows a diagrammatic cross-section of the abdomen of the mantis, with the wings folded at rest. The remigium of the fore wing encloses and protects the hind wing, and the pleats of the hind wing are folded together like a concertina. The crests of the pleats are occupied by the main veins which support the pleats, the troughs being formed by intercalary veins, which are the smaller veins inserted between the main veins.

structure instantly endows it with the ability to bear weight. There is no magic involved. What has happened is that, as a result of the pleats, the stresses imposed by the load have now been taken up by tension in the plane of the paper. Although a sheet of paper cannot resist bending, it has unusual tensile strength as you can easily verify by trying to stretch it between your fingers and thumbs.

How can we apply this analogy to insect wings? Figure 9 shows that if a system of parallel pleats is drawn together at one end to form a fan, the structure achieves even greater bending strength, and the same principle can be seen at work in the expanded hind wing vanes of large insects such as grasshoppers, crickets, cockroaches, stick insects and the mantids that we saw in Chapter 3.

The vane is constructed exactly along the lines of a lady's fan, with pleats radiating out from the base. The comparison is obvious from the moment the vane opens up at the start of flight, as can be seen in high-speed photographs of mantids and grasshoppers unfolding their wings as they leap into the air. Incidentally, the fan-wise opening and closing of the vane over the abdomen at the start and end of flight illustrates another advantage of pleated folding: it enables the insect to pack away a large area of membrane into the minimum space (see Figure 10). But the main advantage must surely be the fact that pleating produces in this delicate, lace-like membrane the strength to resist the stresses that it will experience during flight.

It was Dr Robin Wootton of Exeter University in England who pointed out the full complexity of the design of these fan-like

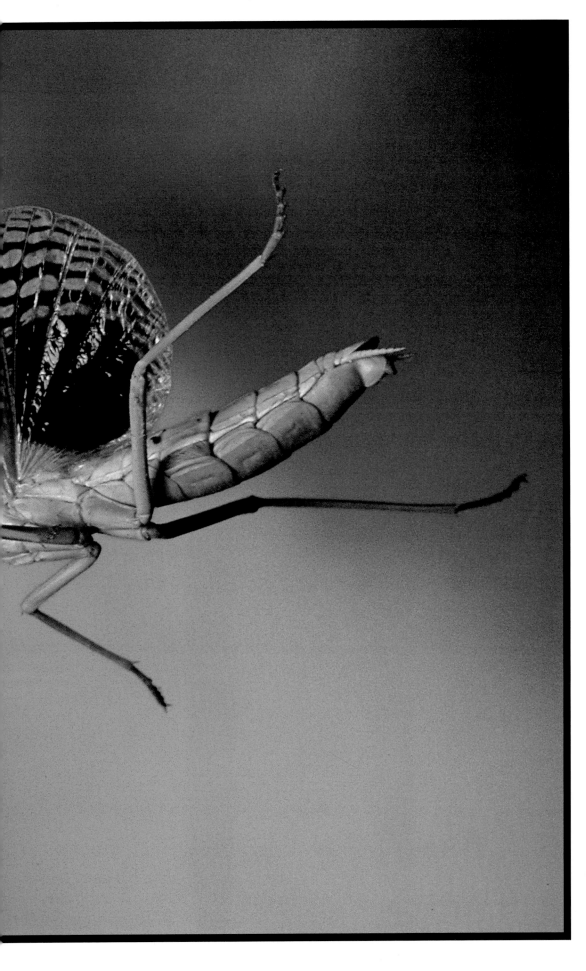

44. The coloured 'eye' in the hind wing of the mantis *Iris oratoria* probably serves the same purpose as flash coloration in grasshoppers (see photograph 95, page 186): distracting a potential aggressor. The wings of the insect shown in this photograph are just beginning their descent.

45. Like mantids, crickets and grasshoppers are often equipped with large pleated hind wings – none more so than the migratory locust *Locusta migratoria*, whose powers of flight are legendary. These two photographs demonstrate the behaviour of the pleats during opposite phases of the stroke cycle. In both cases the flying insect is being viewed directly from below. In **A** the fore and hind wings are both being raised during the upstroke. The inertia of the fore wing tips has caused them to bend downwards as the wing ascends. The hind wing is partially retracted during the upstroke, and this deepens the pleats in the same way that partly closing a lady's fan deepens the folds. The deepening of the pleats stiffens the wing, increasing its resistance to downward bending. In **B,** both wings are beginning the downstroke. The hind wing has been drawn forward and the wing surface is now fully expanded, flattening out the pleats and allowing the vane to develop an umbrella-like camber.

A

B ▶

Figure 11. The main flexion lines of the mantis's fore wing, the claval furrow and the median flexion line, exert a strong influence on its shape during the flight cycle. The flexion lines subdivide the wing into costal, radial and claval sections and permit movements of these sections relative to one another. **A** shows in diagrammatic form the right fore wing, viewed from above, just at the point of lower stroke reversal. At this moment the base of the wing begins to move upwards under the force of the upstroke flight muscles. Owing to its inertia, the wing tip will tend to continue its downward movement. **B** shows what would happen at this moment if there were no compensatory movements taking place between the flexion lines. The entire wing surface, including the base, would experience a strong downward flexure. In fact, what actually happens at the start of the upstroke is that the costal section of the wing swings backwards around the median flexion line, and the radial section simultaneously swings backwards around the claval furrow as shown in **A1.** The result is that the wing instantaneously acquires a strong corrugation which increases its resistance to downward flexure. The corrugation confines the flexure to the region outboard of the claval furrow (**B1**). Near the wing tip the corrugation becomes smoothed out to form a chordwise flexure or reverse camber, which may increase the ability to generate lift and thrust during the

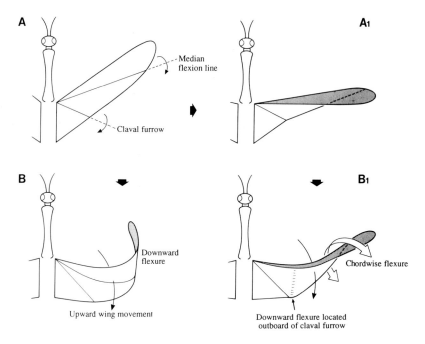

upstroke. The undersides of the wings have been shaded to aid identification.

---

wings. As the wing billows out during the downstroke, the rim of the trailing edge becomes pulled taut but the inner part of the wing remains pleated. Further billowing then forces both the trailing edge and the veins that run along the crests of the pleats to bend downward elastically. The pleats therefore become partially flattened to create a highly efficient cambered aerofoil. The effect is very similar to opening an umbrella.

The importance of flexion lines

When we turn to the front wing of the mantis, we find that it is not pleated like the hind wing, but has two very prominent flexion lines: the median flexion line and the claval furrow. These divide the wing into three sections: costal, radial and claval (see Figure 11). The median flexion line and claval furrow can be identified in the wings of almost all insects and play an important role in controlling changes in wing profile during the stroke cycle. High-speed photography of flying mantids shows that the wing profile is virtually flat during the downstroke and there is little sign of any movement about the flexion lines. It is only after the up-

stroke has begun that the influence of the flexion lines on the dynamics of the wing becomes apparent.

Before considering how the flexion lines work we should first of all note that the front wing of a mantis, in contrast to the hind, is relatively thick although still flexible. It is like a plastic ruler: it will bend if enough force is applied along its length, or at its tip if the base is fixed.

These properties of weight and elasticity have a pronounced effect on the changes in shape of the wing during the stroke cycle. The effects will be most felt at the points of stroke reversal when the wing as a whole must decelerate, stop, then start accelerating in the opposite direction. For instance, at the start of the upstroke the dorsoventral muscles contract and begin to force the base of the wing upwards. But because the outer part of the wing is moving much faster than the inner, its inertia causes it to continue its downward movement: it is as though, for the time being, the tip does not know what the base is doing.

We therefore have a situation in which the base of the wing is moving up whilst its tip is

46. The mechanical stresses imposed on a wing are greatest at the stroke extremes when the wing tips experience a rapid reversal of their movement. This reversal imposes large inertial forces on the wing due to its weight. The effects of these forces on wing shape are evident in this photograph of the mantis *Iris oratoria*. The photograph was taken at the moment of stroke reversal from 'down' to 'up', and the fore wing has been distorted into a propeller-like shape as it begins its motion. This distortion results from downwardly directed bending forces acting along the wing axis, aided by an active twisting of the main part of the wing around the claval furrow. Fuller details of this process are given on page 92 and illustrated in Figure 11. Note that the leading edge of the hind wing has also supinated as the wing begins its upward movement.

still moving down, and the result is that a wave of bending starts to travel inwards along the wing towards its base. The fabric of the main part of the wing is strong enough to withstand any damage from the shearing effect that this might produce, and a lot of the tensile stress is taken up in the veins. But there is a danger that when the wave reaches the base it will tear the softer parts connecting the wing to the body.

An impression of what could happen can be obtained by carrying out a simple experiment using a plastic ruler. Fix 1 cm of one end of the ruler on the edge of a table using your thumb, and with the other thumb pluck the projecting main part of the ruler into vibration. The pressure that you feel at the base of the ruler gives you some idea of the stress that would be experienced in the base of the mantis's wing.

This is where the flexion line comes into play; it stops the flexural wave from invading the base, and it does this in the following manner (see Figure 11). We need to go back to the start of the upstroke. The tip-to-base wave has just begun to move inwards. At the same time we see that the costal and radial sections of the wing suddenly hinge backwards about the median flexion line and claval furrow respectively. As a result, a gutter is formed along the wing, its bottom being the radial section and its front and rear walls being formed by the costal and claval sections. This corrugation behaves in exactly the same way as the pleats in the mantis's hind wing: it increases the bending resistance of the wing. As a result, the flexural wave that began at the wing tip and is moving inwards is suddenly stopped in its tracks by the claval furrow, and the delicate basal articulation of the wing is protected. But the real elegance of the design lies in the fact that none of the wave energy is lost. By the time the wave has been halted at the claval furrow all its energy has been gathered into a pronounced downward bend in the wing at that point. The wing now suddenly snaps back towards its straightened shape and the resultant surge of extra speed in the wing as it moves through the air forces it to generate additional lift.

The advantages of a wing that bends

Various kinds of wing flexure can be seen in insects, and the example quoted is a typical case of the transverse bending that is commonly encountered, particularly in long-winged species. This kind of bending is almost always associated with the lower point of stroke reversal and, therefore, the bending is downward. High-speed photographs show downward wing bending time and time again, but upward bending is seen only occasionally. Insect wings appear to be built to allow one-way bending, a quality that is due at least in part to their natural camber.

47. This photograph of the wasp beetle *Clytus arietis* illustrates downward flexure in the wings during the upstroke.

48. In these two photographs of a flying ichneumon fly *Lampronata* the wings have just begun the downstroke (**A**) and upstroke (**B**) respectively. Downwardly directed bending forces have clearly affected the wings in the latter case, but there is no evidence of any upward flexure of the wing in the former.

49. These two photographs of a green lacewing illustrate the gradual development of downward bending in the wings at the start of the upstroke. In **A,** the fully lowered fore and hind wings show no sign of flexure in their leading edges. In **B,** the fore wings have supinated and begun their ascent. The bending forces on the fore wing at this time have flexed its leading edge downwards.

◄ **A**

B

50. These photographs illustrate downward flexure of the wings during the upstroke phase of the wingbeat in: **A,** scarlet tiger moth *Callimorpha dominula*; **B,** scarce silver lines moth *Bena prasinana*; **C,** seven-spot ladybird beetle *Coccinella 7-punctata* and **D,** lilac beauty moth *Apeira syringaria*.

51. The wings of this hoverfly *Chrysotoxum cautum* (left) have just started their upward movement. When viewed from directly in front (**A**) the wings appear to be straight, but when we see the same phase from obliquely behind (**B**) it is clear that the wing tips have been bent strongly downwards.

Most wings are positively cambered, having a convex upper surface and a concave lower surface. Just like a piece of plastic roof guttering, the wing will bend much more easily to the concave side than it will to the convex side. The wing will bend in response to the downward forces acting along its length during the upstroke, but will resist the upward forces acting along it during the downstroke.

Most of the bending resistance of an insect's wing is located in the leading edge spar, which consists of several long veins grouped or fused together. And, as we have just seen in the mantis's fore wing, the spar can behave like an elastic rod, alternately accumulating elastic energy during one part of the stroke and releasing it to produce more lift during a later part of the stroke.

It is therefore all the more curious, and somewhat surprising, to find that the leading edge spar in the wings of some insects is interrupted halfway along its length by a fracture, the so-called costal break. A costal break can be seen in the wings of mayflies, stoneflies, caddis flies and many Hemiptera, Hymenoptera and Diptera, and the front wing of cicadas has a whole line of similar breaks across the wing, the so-called nodal line.

The purpose of these breaks appears to be to exaggerate the one-way bending properties of the wing, and also to restrict any downward bending to the part of the wing lying outboard of the break. This has the expected beneficial effect of guarding the wing base against mechanical stress, but also allows the wing to adopt the best profile during the stroke.

52. These two photographs illustrate the flexural response of the wings of the yellow shell moth *Camptogramma bilineata* during the upstroke phase of the wing beat cycle. In **A,** (opposite) the wings have just begun the upstroke, and the resultant downwardly directed forces have produced a marked flexure. In **B,** (right) the wings have ascended to the second half of the upstroke and the flexure has nearly disappeared now that the wing tip has caught up with the wing base.

◄ **A**

B

A

53. Flexural distortion of the wings of the ichneumon fly *Ophion luteus*. Many ichneumon flies and other Hymenopterans show a costal break in the veins of the leading edge of the fore wing (see Figure 12). The break consists of a fracture in a locally thickened area or 'stigma', and acts as a one-way hinge permitting downward flexure of the wing tip but not upward. In **A** the wings are exactly level with the body during the downstroke. The costal break can be seen as a white dot halfway along the leading edge, but there is no sign of any upward flexure of the wing. In contrast, there is strong downward flexion of the wing tip in **B** (opposite) as the wings begin to ascend. The flexure is concentrated at the costal break. The fore wing has just supinated, bringing its upper surface to face directly downwards. This inversion of the wing is assisted by the tip flexure, and allows the wing to adopt the best angle of attack as it moves backwards with respect to the body. **C** and **D** (opposite) show a similar comparison of downstroke and upstroke wing characteristics in *Netelia testaceus*.

Figure 12. The fore wings of many Hymenoptera, including the ichneumon fly illustrated here, possess a thickened area or stigma on the leading edge. This stigma is frequently associated with a fracture in the costal margin of the wing. During the upstroke the wing undergoes pronounced downward flexion, mainly located at the costal fracture (see photographs 53A, B, C and D and 54). The hind wing does not have a costal fracture or a stigma. It is also shorter and experiences much less downward distortion during its movement.

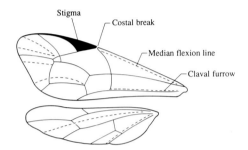

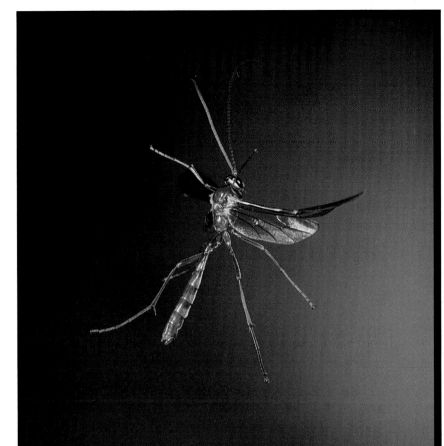

B

C

D

When you first start thinking about the construction of wings in flying animals it seems surprising to find the inclusion of elements deliberately designed to increase deformability. But by now the reader is probably becoming more and more aware that plastic deformability, far from being an embarrassment to the insect's wing, is actually the secret of its strength. In fact the same quality is also built into the wings of modern aircraft, although not to the same degree that we see it in insects. Anyone who has felt the spine-jolting impact of a jet aircraft passing through a pocket of air turbulence will know that air, insubstantial substance though it is, can in certain circumstances take on the properties of concrete. If you had bothered to look out of the window during one of these episodes, you would probably have seen the wing wobbling. This should instil confidence rather than the reverse, because it signifies that much of the impact of the turbulence has been absorbed by the elastic vibration of the wing.

To the many advantages of the insect's flexi-wing can therefore be added the role of shock absorber. But this by no means exhausts the possible list. For example, if a wing undergoes extensive bending during the stroke, its tip travels through a greater arc. It therefore covers a greater distance in the same amount of time – in other words its mean speed relative to the air increases and it generates more lift.

If you examine the photographs of a flying ichneumon fly *Ophion* shown in photographs 53A and B, you will see yet another advantage of the flexi-wing. The fore wing of *Ophion* has a costal break which accentuates its tendency to downward bending at the start of the upstroke. When the insect is taking off, hovering or flying very slowly forward it needs to generate lift on the upstroke as well as the downstroke. This is achieved by supinating the wing on the upstroke, but when this is also combined with downward flexure the angle of attack of the wing can be adjusted to the optimal degree.

54. Downward flexion of the fore wing tip at the start of the upstroke in a saw-fly. Note that, as in the ichneumon fly shown in photograph 53, the flexion is concentrated at the thickened part of the leading edge which contains the costal break.

55. The fore wing of cicadas has a line of weakness or nodal line running across the surface from its leading to its trailing edge. The line consists of a break in several of the long wing veins, including those of the costal margin, and divides the wing into an inner supporting zone and an outer deformable zone. Like the costal break in Hymenopteran wings, the nodal line acts as a one-way hinge. In this flying *Tibicina haematodes* we see that the fore wing is perfectly flat during the downstroke (**A**) but bent strongly downwards along the nodal line during the start of the upstroke (**B**). The nodal line runs between the two arrows on **A**. Note also that the fore wing has supinated and the inner part of the wing is moving backwards with a positive angle of attack. Because of its deformability the wing tip can now adapt its shape to give the best possible angle of attack.

56. The hind wings of many beetles are very large, possibly to compensate for the fact that the fore wings are inactive during flight. In ladybirds such as this seven-spot *Coccinella 7-punctata* the wings are approximately twice as long as the elytra and the abdomen, and must be folded along their length if they are to be stowed away after use. The main line of folding coincides with the division between the heavily reinforced basal region of the wing and the deformable tip, and is clearly seen in **A.**

A

B ▶

57. The fore wings of Heteroptera are divided into an inner leathery region and a smaller outer membranous region (see Figures 2 and 13). These two photographs (left) of a flying shield bug *Palomena* show downward flexure of the membranous wing tip during the upstroke. **A** is a view from above the insect, **B** from below. In **B**, note how the expanded inner or claval part or the hind wing clings to the undersides of the abdomen. A similar thing occurs in Lepidopteran flight as discussed in Chapter 7.

58. Some species of Heteropteran bug have a cuneal fracture in the leathery part of the fore wing, and this influences wing shape during flight. Like the costal break of Hymenopterans or the nodal line of cicadas, the cuneal fracture appear to work like a one-way hinge. In these photographs of a flying *Leptoterna* we see evidence of downward flexure of the wing tips during the early (**A,** right) and later stages (**B,** opposite) of the upstroke. Figure 13 is a drawing from this photograph.

B

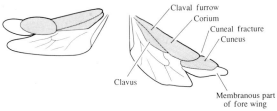

Figure 13. Drawing of the wings of the flying bug *Leptoterna*, taken directly from photograph 58B. The wings are halfway through the upstroke. Note the slight downward flexure of the fore wing at the cuneal fracture.

Claval furrow
Corium
Cuneal fracture
Cuneus
Clavus
Membranous part of fore wing

59. As this soldier beetle *Cantharis* prepares for flight we see the still crumpled wing tips which are normally folded back upon the main part of the wing when not in use. There must be a mechanism that allows the tip to be fully 'ironed-out' when the beetle launches into flight.

A

B

60. These photographs of a flying soldier beetle *Cantharis rustica* show how autoregulation of wing tip shape takes place during flight in beetles. In **A** the wings are starting their downstroke, and the air pressure beneath the wings has flattened out the main fold in the tip. In **B** the wings have reversed their movement and are beginning the upstroke. The pressure is now greater on the upper side of the wing tip than the lower and has forced it to fold downwards.

61. The mechanism described in the caption to photographs 60A and B is also at work in this longhorn beetle *Agapanthea villosoviridescens.* In **A** the wings are beginning their downstroke and the wing tips are perfectly flat. In **B,** as the wings begin their upstroke the tip has become folded downwards under the pressure acting upon its upper surface.

◀**A**   **B**

Veins and plumes

The wing veins are primarily responsible for imparting elastic strength to the wing, but they are not all equally indispensable in this role. Vein reduction can be recognized as a clear trend in groups such as the fungus midges (family Cecidomyiidae) and the tiny parasitic wasps known collectively as chalcids. In some chalcids little remains of the veins other than a thickening of the leading edge, and this appears to be the minimum requirement for a functioning wing. Compare this with the 'primitive' venation pattern of insects such as the ant-lion and lacewing shown in photographs 62A and B. Here the wings carry a dense network of cross-veins, and the main long veins fork profusely near the margin of the wing.

A

B ▶

62. The giant ant-lion *Palpares libelloides* (**A**) and the lacewing *Chrysopa perla* (**B**) both display a 'primitive' pattern of wing venation. The long veins fork near the wing margin and there is a dense network of cross-veins, giving rise to the name of the order to which the ant-lions and lacewings belong: Neuroptera or 'nerve-winged' insects.

A

63. Plume moths of the family
Pterophoridae have wings
that are divided into a series
of feather-like segments, each
consisting of a slender, hair-
fringed shaft. This design
produces a lighter wing but
does not seem to alter its
structural qualities or the way
it deforms during flight, as
these photographs illustrate.
In **A** the wings are fully
raised above the body at the
start of the downstroke, and
the leading edge of the fore
wing is straight. In **B,** at the
start of the upstroke, the
leading edge of the fore wing
has been flexed downwards
along its entire length. Note
that there is no sign of flexure
in the three plumes making
up the hind wing because
they are much shorter than
those of the fore wing and
therefore experience less
inertial loading during the
stroke reversal.

Reduction of a different kind can be seen in the wings of thunder-flies (order Thysanoptera), various families of micro-moths and tiny chalcids belonging to the family Mymaridae, the so-called fairy flies. The hind wings of these insects, and in some cases also the fore wings, consist of nothing but a slender shaft fringed with microscopic hairs. These hairs represent what would otherwise be continuous wing membrane, and the reasons for this curious adaptation have been the subject of much controversy.

Until fairly recently it was argued that these 'plumed' wings enabled very small insects to 'swim' through the air, by using the air's viscosity rather than its density.

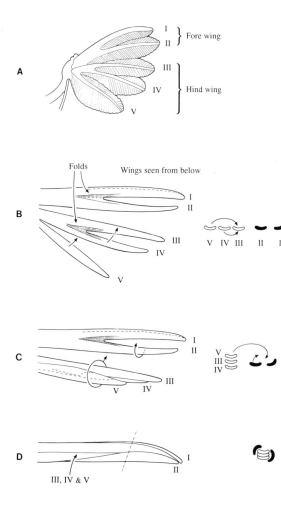

Figure 14. The wings of plume moths are divided into feathered segments, usually two in the fore wing and three in the hind wing. During flight, as shown in **A,** the plumes are spread apart like the fingers of a hand. When at rest, some species are able to fold the plumes together so that they resemble a twig. **B, C** and **D** illustrate the complex way in which this folding is achieved. The fringes of hair on the wing segments have been omitted for clarity. The shaft of each plume is flattened and slightly bevelled, as shown in the diagrammatic cross-sections of the wings on the right. Plumes I and II of the fore wing are divided by a fold which corresponds to the claval furrow found in most insect wings. A similar fold is formed between plumes III and IV of the hind wing. Plume V is divided almost completely from the rest of the hind wing. The flattened, blade-like shape of the plumes of the hind wing, together with the great flexibility of their bases, allows them to fold together like a motor mechanic's 'feeler gauge', or a set of keys on a ring. This process is illustrated in **B.** As a result, plume III comes to lie in the middle with plumes IV and V above and below respectively. The folded plumes of the hind wing are now drawn forward and enclosed between plumes I and II of the fore wing. The resulting bundle of plumes is only a fraction of the width of the fully spread wing.

Presumably the proponents of this idea had in mind as a model the tiny water-flea *Daphnia* which propels itself through pond-water by beating its feathery antennae-like wings. It now seems more likely that plumed wings behave just like any other wing; the hairs probably produce a rather lighter wing, but they are so closely packed together that they present an effectively unbroken surface to the air. Air flows 'across' the hairs, but not 'through' them. Perhaps this should come as no surprise since it is exactly what we find in a bird's feather. A flight feather consists almost entirely of a dense feltwork of microscopic, hooked hairs; but, again, air flows across the pile, not through it.

Feather-like wings are not restricted to the smallest of insects; one of the most interesting examples occurs in the plume moths, which often measure up to 2–3 cm in wing-span. The wings of these insects are deeply dissected into a series of plumes, usually two in the front and three in each hind wing. The plumed design produces a reduction in weight but not at the expense of strength or wing area. But it also enables the wings to be furled at rest in a way that would be impossible in a continuous, flat wing.

The basis of the folding mechanism is remarkably similar to that of a motor engineer's feeler gauge, as illustrated in Figure 14. A feeler gauge consists of a stack of thin blades which open and close like a fan. Each blade can be likened to a single segment of the plume moth's wings. When the plumes of the wing have been furled in this fashion the wing comes to resemble a narrow, thorn-like object, similar in size and shape to the body. It is a very effective piece of camouflage because the insect normally rests suspended amongst vegetation and, aided by its cryptic coloration, takes on the appearance of a three-pronged thorn. I am not aware of this kind of wing folding in any other insect group, although the clefts in the wing separating off the different plumes coincide with the flexion lines seen in continuous wings. In this sense, plume moths seem to have achieved the ultimate form of wing 'flexibility' by eroding away the flexion lines until nothing is left but a gap.

64. In the world of insects, dragonflies are the embodiment of speed, power and control in flight. The huge thorax indicates the size and strengh of the flight muscles. This *Aeschna cyanea* is counterstroking the wings: the front and hind pairs are beating half a cycle out of phase.

· 5 ·

SPEED, POWER AND FLIGHT CONTROL

In Chapter 2 we looked in detail at the working parts of the flight machine without spending much time examining its performance characteristics. This is rather like providing the prospective purchaser of a car with a blueprint of its engine design when what he or she really wants to know is how the car performs on the road. When we do examine the flight performance of insects in the field we soon discover that there are as many variations in power, controllability and technique as there are different insect groups. One generality that can safely be made, however, is that power naturally accompanies speed. At its simplest, we can see this in the difference in flight habit between a cranefly cruising along, legs lazily dangling below, and a dragonfly or hawkmoth cleaving a path swiftly through the air.

It would be wrong to try to draw too close a comparison between 'high performance' insect fliers, such as dragonflies and drone-flies, and man-made machines like aircraft, but such a comparison could not have been far from the mind of an individual quoted by the eminent German zoologist Werner Nachtigall. Nachtigall demolished a report appearing in a scientific journal that a bot-fly had been sighted at the top of a mountain in New Mexico flying at an estimated speed of 1300 km per hour! This exceeds the speed of sound and, as Nachtigall noted, the poor insect's head would have been squashed flat by the sheer pressure of the air. Once again science triumphs over the imagination, but the original observer should not be too dismayed: at an altitude of twelve thousand feet anyone can be forgiven a little exaggeration!

The speed of flight
There can be no doubt, however, that botflies and their kindred blow-flies, hoverflies and bee-flies are remarkable performers, capable of bursts of speeds in excess of 40 km per hour: this is faster, for instance, than the world record speed for sprinting the men's 100 metres. Large hawker dragonflies and hawkmoths can muster speeds of up to 60 km per hour, keeping abreast of even the fleetest hedgerow birds. Stooping falcons and diving swifts can better this performance with the help of gravity, but it is noteworthy that comparable diving flight is rarely shown by insects – although butterflies are an exception, as we shall see later in this chapter.

Mention of the word 'horsefly' causes most people instinctively to cringe with dislike (not least the author), and no one who has been pursued by these insects will find it hard to accept that they can fly at speeds of at least 20 km per hour – depending on appetite, of course! This reminds me of an occasion when my wife and I were toiling up a grassy mountain slope in the French Pyrenees on a hot, sunny day. Suddenly, as though the heavens had opened, we were besieged by a squadron of these insects. They were of the huge tabanid variety and resemble nothing so much as a bullet in size, shape, hardness and instant foreboding. I distinctly remember my wife screaming as she beat a retreat down the mountainside. We finally beat off the attack, but only with the help of walking sticks. Later I came to the conclusion that these bombastic creatures are mainly interested in people as objects of sport, although that thought would have comforted neither of us at the time.

Experience has not dampened my dislike for the notorious cleg-fly *Haematopota* or the equally aggressive but beautiful golden-eyed *Chrysops*, both of which are the real menace to man. These two become frenzied at the merest waft of human perspiration, and serious attacks have left people questioning the madness of putting men and flies on the earth together. Although their flight is slower than that of the tabanids, they make their approach silently from behind. Clegs are said to prefer the nape of the neck, but in my experience they choose the spots where the skin is stretched more thinly over bony prominences such as the inside knob of the elbow, the knobs on either side of the wrist, and the variety of tuberosities around the shoulder. I have found that the only practical way to stay alert to their attentions, especially when you are on the move, is to keep a regular eye on your own shadow on the ground: for when an insect is approaching from behind it may be possible to detect its shadow even though you cannot see the insect itself.

When discussing the subject of flight speeds in insects, biologists are often tempted to draw direct parallels with other animals such as flying birds or running mammals, but since insects are so much smaller than the rest this is not a fair comparison. This problem of scale can be overcome by discussing speeds in terms of the number of body lengths that a moving animal covers in a given amount of time. On this basis, insects score very heavily, top marks going to the humble housefly which clocks up about 250 body lengths per second. Men and hares manage a mere five or six body lengths, and even diving swifts do only moderately well in comparison with houseflies, with a score of eighty. By whatever standards we chose to judge them, using a weighted scale or simply measuring their absolute speed through the air, insects are very impressive flying machines.

But why is speed important? This is not a particularly easy question to answer. Ask

65. Robber flies lie in wait for their prey and take it on the wing using the 'capture-dart' technique. This relies on lightning powers of acceleration. The specimen shown has just caught a small species of cicada, which it is restraining with its powerful legs. Note the large, domed thorax housing the huge flight muscles.

yourself the same question: 'Is speed important to me when I move?' One answer is that if the purpose of the movement is to travel over a large distance from A to B then I will take the fastest means available, in order to save time. However this is not necessarily the logic that an insect would use. When travelling from A to B a particular insect may decidedly *not* want to travel as fast as possible, for fear of missing opportunities for feeding or mating that may present themselves on the way. Also, the insect may be less concerned with speed and more concerned with getting to its destination with the least use of energy. These two are not necessarily the same thing. The insect must decide how to balance the energy that will be used against the time that will be taken and the opportunities that may be lost or gained.

As everyone knows, given the choice between running a mile and walking a mile, most people would choose to walk because it is easier and seems less tiring. This approach, of course, wouldn't do if you had to catch a bus. Insects are probably no different from ourselves in this respect: they will adapt their behaviour to the problem before them, and will usually keep something in reserve for a genuine emergency.

Insect migration
One particular situation where speed might be thought to be important is migration. This applies to birds as well as insects, but also to large herds of mammals such as wildebeest and to travelling Bedouin tribesmen. The occasions when migrating animals need to travel continuously at speed are relatively few: birds crossing maritime straits are an obvious example. More often than not an observer might be in the midst of a group of moving animals without even knowing that they were migrating. The group might be foraging, and drifting steadily in a prevailing direction, but at any one moment the observer might find it difficult to predict which.

An analogy could be drawn with the behaviour of a flock of rooks. In early summer fledgling rooks, testing out their wings, make sorties away from the rookery and then slowly return along a drawn-out spiral route. Similar spiralling behaviour can be observed in cranes and birds of prey as they soar downwind. At any given moment the heads of these animals will be pointed in any compass direction, yet they are all travelling in only one direction.

Endurance is probably a more valuable asset to a migrating animal than either power or speed, although of course a modicum of all three is necessary. Amongst insects, for example, butterflies, ladybirds and aphids are all capable of migrating over fairly long distances, yet they are not the most powerful fliers. Even locusts, the proverbial insect migrants, fly at only a modest speed of 15 km per hour without a wind to assist them. Migrating insects rely a great deal on their instinctive ability to 'read' the prevailing weather conditions, and time their launch accordingly. A swarm of locusts seems to possess a collective intelligence that enables it to exploit winds and thermals in order to gain height. From altitude the swarm can then obtain a 'free lift' by gliding across country for several kilometres with little use of energy.

Migrating butterflies also use thermals to transport them to the level of, and sometimes into, the cloud base, where they may then find themselves in the company of soaring birds and, not unusually, glider pilots. In fact much of the information we possess on migrating insects, particularly butterflies, is due to the incidental observations made by glider pilots. It has been estimated, for instance, that each kilometre of altitude gained by a migrating monarch butterfly allows it to glide 4 km across country before it finally descends back to its original level. The butterflies can also use 'slope lift' produced by wind blowing across rising terrain. The effect is most pronounced at a point halfway up the slope, and it is at precisely this level that the insects have been observed to rest their wings and continue to soar upwards.

The other main advantage to be gained by soaring to high altitude is that it increases the chances of being caught up in more rapidly moving airstreams. Of course the insect cannot choose where the airstream is going, but as long as dispersal *per se* is a more important priority than migrating towards a specific target area the technique can yield large dividends. Swarms of locusts occasionally make landfall in the Caribbean islands after being carried from breeding grounds in North Africa, several thousand miles to the east. Journeys of this magnitude could not possibly be achieved by continuous powered flight, and the only explanation seems to be that such swarms have been fortuitously transported by high altitude jet-streams. But it seems equally likely that, for each swarm that successfully reaches its destination, many must be dispatched without trace into the open sea.

Migration has been studied in detail in only a relatively few, mostly economically important, insects but the migratory instinct is probably widespread in the group. Many species migrate only locally, restricting their movements to within a few kilometres of their original breeding grounds and travelling inside the so-called boundary layer. This is the zone of relatively mild winds close to the ground, where the insect's flight speed will often exceed the wind speed. Although insects migrating within the boundary layer will usually follow a particular compass direction, such as north–south, they will also navigate using landmarks such as roads, rivers and the coastline if these head in the same general direction. Once the insect leaves the boundary layer it is almost entirely at the mercy of the elements, since the wind speed will usually be much greater than its own 'still-air' flight speed.

The 4000 km migrations undertaken annually by North American monarch butterflies from their breeding grounds in southern Ontario in Canada to their overwintering quarters in Mexico are far more impressive feats than the transatlantic journeys made by locusts since, as far as we can tell, they involve a far more regulated pattern of behaviour. Yet here again, a simple calculation shows that the butterfly could not achieve its goal without the aid of the elements.

The average weight of a pre-migratory monarch butterfly is about 600 mg (almost exactly one-fiftieth of an ounce!), of which 150 mg is fat manufactured out of dietary nectar. If all the fat was burned as fuel for the flight muscles, it would allow the butterfly to travel non-stop for about forty-four hours. Assuming that the butterfly cruised at an average speed of 18 km per hour, without wind assistance, its maximum range would therefore be in the region of 800 km. This is a long way short of the actual distance covered. Either the butterflies must be putting down in order to feed *en route*, and perhaps losing valuable time in the process, or they must be capitalizing on good meteorological conditions.

What we know about the flight behaviour of butterflies suggests that they are indeed eminently capable of reading the weather and riding the winds to their advantage. At its simplest, this means using tail winds to boost forward speed even though, as yachtsmen will tell you, a tail wind generates speed at the expense of control. Butterflies are confident fliers and will readily take on head winds or cross winds, often stooping to within a metre or so of the ground to avoid the fastest currents.

They also use special techniques for crossing obstacles in a head wind such as mountain ridges, buildings and walls. As the butterfly approaches the obstacle from downwind it hugs the ground, beating hard with its wings until it reaches the relative calm at the base of the obstacle. From there it begins a nearly vertical climb through the relatively still air. The butterfly braces itself for the full force of the wind as it reaches the summit, again hugs the ground to make the summit traverse, then descends as quickly as possible to lower ground on the other side, often diving like a hawk with wings closed or held in a V-configuration above the body. Readers may be able to recognize similar elements of flight behaviour as butterflies pass through their gardens on bright, breezy days, particularly if the garden is surrounded by high walls or fences.

The cost of speed

Although stamina and technique may easily compensate for any deficiencies in outright speed and power in a migrating insect, there are unquestionably instances where these latter qualities dominate flight. Robber flies (family Asilidae) are a good example. These flies hunt their prey using the 'capture-dart' method which relies on being able to spring from hiding, seize the victim and return to the same spot all within the space of a second or two at most. The manoeuvre calls for perfect timing and exceptional powers of acceleration. Large species such as *Asilus crabroniformis* and *Laphria flava* are recognizable by their characteristically humped thorax housing the huge flight muscles necessary to power these accelerations. The high-speed manoeuvre is very costly in energy terms and is used, understandably, only in bursts.

Paradoxically, hawkmoths and bees do not seem to be governed by the same restriction, since they appear to be able to maintain high levels of flight activity almost continuously. Possibly the difference lies in the fact that foraging bees and hawkmoths are continuously refreshed by the rapidly digestible nectar that they imbibe. Also, looked at from a logistics point of view, almost every 'strike' that a bee or hawkmoth makes is a lucky one because each flower will yield some nectar. In contrast the robber fly, no matter how cleverly it performs, will never achieve a hit rate of more than, say, one in five – and in many cases it will be much lower than this.

It could be argued that bees and moths spend a lot of their time hovering, rather than accelerating forwards, and that this would make their flight more economical. To this it can be answered that we still do not know which is more expensive, forward flight or hovering, although in theory at least the mechanical drag on an insect's wings and body should diminish as it flies faster. The problem of energy use by animals flying at different speeds is of considerable interests to zoologists, particularly in relation to migration. Each species of insect, bird or bat can fly within a given range of speeds, but within that range there may not be a great deal of difference in the rate at which they consume energy.

This means that there may not be any particular speed at which it is most economical for the animal to fly. Naturally there is an upper limit to absolute flight speed, which varies with species, but below this limit it is possible that the animal is free to choose its speed without incurring any energy penalty. This is very important because it means that the animal can afford to indulge in the full range of its flying abilities, for 'play' as well as for more serious purposes, without having to worry all the time about how much energy it is using.

The timing of the wing beat
When we look at movement in terrestrial, as opposed to flying, animals we find that it is impossible to talk about walking or running speed without at the same time taking into account changes in gait. Most people will be familiar with the fact that a horse picks up speed as it moves through a succession of gaits from a walk to a trot to a canter and finally a gallop. Each of these gaits involves a different rhythm of the legs and a progressive reduction in the amount of time the feet spend in contact with the ground.

Amongst four-legged animals as a whole there are at least a dozen or so possible gaits, although no single animal displays the whole range. Lizards can trot, but no one will be surprised to know that tortoises cannot gallop! Being able to match speed to gait is an extremely useful device for a running animal because it permits maximum ease and economy of movement, just like using the gears of a car.

Human beings have only two natural gaits, walking and running. Although unnatural gaits such as one- or two-legged hopping and skipping can be acquired, they are extraordinarily inefficient and totally impractical as a means of transport. Birds in flight have only one gait: simultaneous flapping of both wings. Curiously, the obvious theoretical alternative gait for birds, flapping one wing and then the other, appears to be impossible for them to perform

66. Ant-lions (opposite) beat the fore and hind wings out of phase by almost a full half cycle, the fore wings leading the hind. As a result there are moments in the cycle when one wing is pronated and descending whilst the other is supinated and ascending. Out-of-phase beating like this is called counter-stroking. In **A,** showing a species of *Euroleon*, both wing pairs are rising but the fore wings have reached the end of the stroke whilst the hind wings are just starting. A fraction of a second later, as shown in the unidentified species in **B,** the fore wings have pronated and are moving down whilst the hind wings are still supinated and moving up.

even as a specialized manoeuvre. Even human beings can use their arms alternately in propulsion, as in the swimming stroke known as the crawl, and it is also the normal way in which the arms are swung during walking and running.

Returning now to insects we are entitled to ask, since most of them have four wings in all, if they too are capable of changing gait during flight. Again, we must be careful to define exactly what we mean by gait. Clearly the wings of each pair, fore or hind, are absolutely constrained to move together because of the nature of the mechanical linkage with the thorax. The question of gait therefore reduces to whether or not the fore and hind wing pairs can be moved out of phase with one another, or out of beat.

The degree of independent movement that takes place between the wing pairs is determined by the physical coupling, if any, that exists between them. Sometimes the coupling is very loose: for example in butterflies the trailing edge of the fore wing simply overlaps the leading edge of the hind wing. Other members of the Lepidoptera

increase the strength of this linkage by employing two rows of interlocking hairs, one on the lower surface of the trailing edge of the fore wing, the other on the upper surface of the leading edge of the hind wing. These hook together rather like the man-made material Velcro.

Some moths have taken this principle a stage further by gathering the hairs on the leading edge of the hind wing into a more substantial bundle or even fusing them to form a stout bristle. This then engages a catch on the wing in front, in a kind of 'hook and eye' arrangement. In Hymenoptera (wasps, bees, ants and saw-flies) the costal, or leading, edge of the hind wing is sometimes set with a row of hooks which catch on to a fold on the trailing edge of the fore wing.

Another type of wing coupling is shown in the true bugs or Heteroptera. The trailing edge of the fore wing is extended into a triangular flap or clavus which overlaps the hind wing. A short, hair-fringed gutter runs along the underside of the clavus and this engages the costal margin of the hind wing.

67. Counterstroking is the normal pattern of wing beating in damselflies and dragonflies. This picture shows a common blue damselfly *Enallagma cyathigerum*, both wing pairs are supinated and moving upwards. The fore wings have almost reached the end of the stroke but the hind wings are just beginning. Note the pronounced downward flexion of the hind wings.

68. As in the flight of ant lions, dragonflies and damselflies, the fore wings of lacewings preceed the hind wings by about a quarter to half a cycle. The cycle begins in **A** with the hind wings fully lowered near the start of the upstroke. The fore wings are already roughly a third of the way through their upward movement. Note that both wing pairs are supinated. In photograph **B** both wing pairs are continuing their upward movement. In **C** the fore wings have just passed the summit of their stroke, have already pronated and are beginning to move down. The hind wings have not quite reached the top of their stroke and are still supinated.

69. Scorpion flies also exemplify counterstroking, in which the fore and hind wings move out of phase by half a cycle. These three photographs of *Panorpa communis* illustrate stages in the upstroke corresponding almost exactly with those shown in the lacewing in photographs 68A, B, and C.

A

B

C

Mechanisms to ensure wing coupling are so widespread amongst insects that we must begin to conclude that wings often work best when they move together as a single effective surface. Yet if this is the case why have so few groups of insects taken the idea to its limits, as the true flies or Diptera appear to have done, and aborted the hind wings altogether? After all, this completely eliminates any possibility of one pair of wings interfering with the movements of the other. Unquestionably, some of the most powerful and versatile aerial performances are seen in members of the Diptera.

But as we saw earlier in this chapter, there is far more to flight than power and acrobatics. There must be good reasons why many insects have not only retained two pairs of equally effective wings but also move them in a completely independent manner. This kind of locomotion can be seen in lacewings, scorpion flies, alder flies, snake flies, mantids, bush-crickets and grasshoppers, all of which have only loosely coupled or completely uncoupled fore and hind wings which can be seen to move out of phase with one another.

Usually the fore wings are timed to rise and fall ahead of the hind wings. This is equally the case whether we are talking about insects with coupled or uncoupled wings, and implies that the control of flight movements from the command centre of the brain is biased towards the fore wings. In a very strict sense, therefore, the fore wings do indeed 'lead' the hind wings.

Interestingly, we can also see the same order within the movements of each wing itself: the leading edge of the wing moves in advance of the trailing edge. However, in this case the delay in the movement of the trailing edge is due not to nervous control but to physical factors inherent in the construction of the wing. The leading edge is almost invariably stiffened by fusion of veins, whereas the rest of the wing is pliable like an elastic membrane. As a result, if the leading edge is suddenly pulled down or up, as it is at the start of the downstroke or upstroke respectively, the rear section of the wing automatically lags behind in its

movement in the same way that a banner waved in the air follows the movement of the banner staff. The banner analogy is a useful one, because the beating wings of many insects visibly ripple as a wave of deformation spreads through from the leading to the trailing edge. It is necessary to employ very high-speed photography to visualize this movement and butterflies provide a perfect example, as will be seen in Chapter 7.

Knowing that the fore wing usually precedes the hind wing in its movement, and bearing in mind that a wave of elastic movement also travels across each wing from its leading to its trailing edge, we are now entitled to ask a further question. Is it possible that the brain of the insect times the motion of the hind wing so that it rises and falls exactly in harmony with the elastic wave travelling through the fore wing?

Returning again to the banner analogy, this is the same as taking a second banner, holding it behind the first and waving it out of phase with the first so that a continuous wave of movement passes through both surfaces. If you tried to do this in practice you would find it difficult, if not impossible, to get the timing of the movements of the two banner staffs right. All this could be avoided by sewing the second banner staff directly on to the rear edge of the first banner flag. If you now waved this 'double banner' you would see that a continuous wave travels through its entire length, and that the second banner is now perfectly 'coupled' to the movements of the first.

'Waves' in mantis wings

This is an intriguing model of the way insects control the movements of their wings, but is it an accurate one? There is evidence that at least in some groups this may be the case, and the following illustration is taken from studies that I have made on the mantis wing.

The hind wing of a mantis is a wonderful example of lightweight structural design. When you observe its movements with the aid of high-speed photography you are struck above all by the sheer amount of wave-like

Figure 15. This diagram, reconstructed from original photographs, compares the sequence of movements of the fore and hind wings of a lacewing with the movements and shape changes taking place in the hind wing of a mantis. The fore and hind wings of the lacewing move independently, the fore leading the hind by about half a cycle. The mantis's hind wing consists of a thickened front part (remigium) and a membranous vane behind. The vane lags behind the remigium during the stroke cycle. Consequently the front and rear parts of the mantis's hind wing behave like the front and hind wings of the lacewing. Small arrows on the wings signify the direction of the movement of the wings. For identification, the leading edges of the wings of the lacewing have been spotted with a semi-circle.

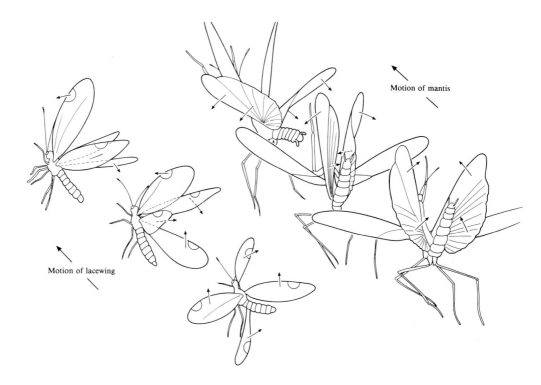

Motion of mantis

Motion of lacewing

motion occurring within its surface. It is difficult to equate the delicacy of this structure with the fact that it generates tremendous aerodynamic force; in fact the hind wing generates about twice the force produced by the much stiffer but narrower fore wing. The sail of a boat is also a limp and useless sheet of canvas when it is suspended in still air, but as soon as it catches the wind it becomes transformed into a structure possessing immense tensile strength, even though it continues to 'flap'.

The wave-like distortions that take place in the mantis's hind wing are an integral part of the way in which it works, and we can understand how the waves come about if we carefully analyse the structure of the wing. The wing is divided into a relatively stiff, narrow section at the front and an expanded, highly pleated section behind, called the vane. The pleats of the vane radiate outwards from the base of the wing like the folds of a lady's fan. The pleats stiffen the wing in the radial direction, but at the same time allow great flexibility to any wave-like motion travelling through the wing from its leading to its trailing edge.

The stiffened front part of the wing, also known as the remigium, articulates at its base with the wing pivot on the thorax. During flight, movements of the thoracic plates are transmitted directly to the remigium, which can therefore be likened to the banner-staff in the model presented above. The vane represents the material of the banner itself. The movement of the hind wing is 'led' by the remigium and the vane 'follows' in turn.

Let us examine the consequences of this serial movement of the different parts of the wing at the start of the downstroke. The remigium begins its descent and at the same time pronates. Successive pleats of the vane then follow suit, and a wave of descent and pronation spreads through the entire vane towards the trailing edge. A consequence of this wave-like motion is that there will be moments during the stroke cycle when the leading and trailing edges of the wing are moving in opposite directions (up or down) and have opposite inclination. This situation is illustrated in Figure 15. If you draw an imaginary dividing line between the remigium and the vane you might almost conclude that they were behaving like two separate wings which were coupled in their movements, the fore wing always leading the hind wing.

Figure 16. This diagrammatic comparison of movements in the wings of a lacewing and in a mantis wing should be studied in conjunction with Figure 15. As in that diagram the leading edges of the wings of the lacewing have been marked with open dots for ease of identification, and filled dots have been located on the corresponding parts of the mantis's hind wing. The insects are drawn as though seen directly from behind.

It would therefore be interesting to take this notion a stage further by making a direct comparison between the movements that we see in the component parts of the mantis's hind wing and the movements of the physically separated fore and hind wings of an insect such as a lacewing. Figure 16 shows the results of such a comparison. We see that the front wing of a lacewing beats in advance of the hind wing, in the same way that the remigium of the mantis's wing leads the vane. We can also identify the same points in

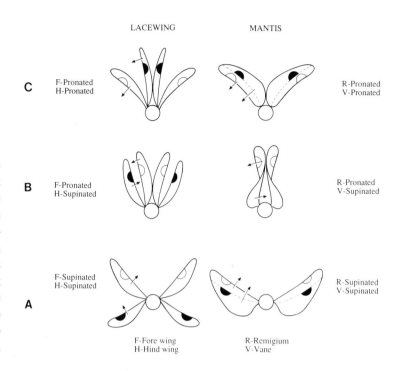

LACEWING   MANTIS

C   F-Pronated   R-Pronated
    H-Pronated   V-Pronated

B   F-Pronated   R-Pronated
    H-Supinated   V-Supinated

A   F-Supinated   R-Supinated
    H-Supinated   V-Supinated

F-Fore wing   R-Remigium
H-Hind wing   V-Vane

A

70. We saw in Figure 10 and photograph 42 that the hind wings of mantids are divided into a leathery remigium forming the leading edge and a large membranous vane behind. The hind wings of crickets and grasshoppers have the same structure. During the stroke these two parts behave almost independently, like the separate fore and hind wings of other insects. In the rear view of a flying mantis shown in **A** (opposite) the front wing and the remigium of the hind wing have both pronated and are beginning their descent. The hind wing vane, however, is still supinated and travelling upwards. **B** (right) shows a similar case, a flying migratory locust *Locusta migratoria*. The fore wing and the hind wing remigium have just supinated and are beginning the upstroke (the left hind wing remigium is seen edge-on and is moving directly outward towards the viewer). But the hind wing vane is still pronated and has not yet reached the bottom of its trajectory.

B

the stroke cycle of the lacewing when the front wing is pronated and moving down whilst simultaneously the hind wing is supinated and moving up. It is as if, despite the fact that the lacewing's fore and hind wings are separated, they are actually being timed to move relative to one another like a single undulating surface.

How insects turn in flight

The discussion in this chapter so far have been mainly concerned with mechanisms that promote speed, power and efficiency of flight in insects, but none of these would be of any use without the appropriate level of control. A person would be unwise to invest a lot of money in a high performance sports

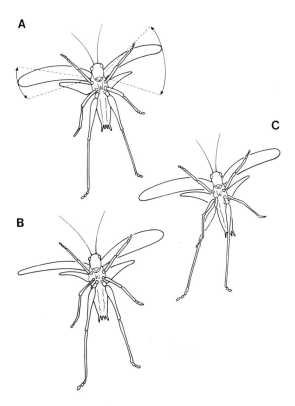

Figure 17. Three ways in which a flying insect can perform a turn. The insect is viewed from in front and in each case it wishes to turn to its right. In **A** and **B** extra power is delivered by the left-hand side wings by increasing either their stroke amplitude (**A**) or the angle of attack (**B**). In both cases the insect makes a banked turn to its right. In **C**, both left and right wing pairs deliver the same power, but slewing the hind legs to the right increases the drag on that side and causes the insect to turn without banking.

car if they were not absolutely certain that they had the speed of reflex to control it. In any moving vehicle, animal or man-made, control resides largely in the ability to make rapid accelerations and decelerations, to negotiate tight turns at speed, and to brake hard.

We can say little about high-speed steering in insects except that it obviously does take place to a phenomenal degree. However, working from first principles and from rather meagre data obtained from insects in slow flight, we can at least fill in some of the gaps.

The first point to be made is that an insect can only turn in the air if it has a means to produce more aerodynamic force on one side of its body than on the other. Theoretically this could be done by beating, say, the left-side wings faster than the right but, as we know, in practice the two wings of a pair must beat together at the same rate. Nevertheless, it is interesting that birds and bats are also incapable of beating the opposite wings at different rates, even though in these cases the movements of the wings are not constrained by mechanical linkages with the body. Birds can obviously move their wings independently when they are preening, but during flight another control programme evidently takes over, rigidly tying their movements together.

Curiously, goldfish are far more resourceful than birds, bats or insects in the ways in which they can move their pectoral fins, which are the anatomical equivalents of wings. If you carefully observe a goldfish swimming in its bowl you will notice that it performs most of its movements not with its body or its tail, but with its pectoral fins. Moreover you will see that, depending on the turns that it wishes to make, it can move the left and right fins at independent rates, backwards or forwards.

Although there can be no difference in the beat between the wings of the two sides of the body of an insect, imbalances of force can still be produced by differentially altering the stroke angle and/or the angle of attack of the wings. An unusual case has been described in the Australian field

71. In this photograph the mantis is making a turning manoeuvre to its left (right as viewed by the reader). Note that the movement of the hind wing vane is being impeded by the left hind leg. As a result, it is likely that the left wings will generate less lift than the right, helping to secure the appropriate turning movement.

cricket *Teleogryllus oceanicus*. When the insect wants to turn, say, to the right, it extends its right hind leg to the side, making it interfere with the motion of the right hind wing. As a result, the left wing produces more force than the right and the right turn is accomplished. We apparently see a similar mechanism at work in the flying mantis shown in photograph 71. Flying locusts use their hind legs, as well as their highly flexible abdomen, as a rudder and presumably this

method can also be put to use by many of the long-legged insects belonging to the orders Diptera, Orthoptera, Hemiptera and Coleoptera. Perhaps the easiest way to produce turning is to increase or decrease the angle of attack of the wings on one side of the body compared to the other. Unfortunately, the changes in lift resulting from this technique also force the insect to roll into the turn: banked turns seem to be the norm in insects, just as they are in aircraft.

72. The wings of this red underwing moth *Catocala nupta* have just come into contact above the body at the end of the upstroke. For a brief moment the wings have ceased to move, consequently no force is being created.

· 6 ·

FORCES OUT OF 'THIN' AIR

Flight is such an extraordinary phenomenon compared to other forms of movement that it is very difficult to understand exactly what it means at the physical level. The fact that we live in an age of air travel probably makes little difference to our general appreciation of the phenomenon. Most of us simply take it for granted that a metal box can suspend itself in the air against gravity without ever questioning the astounding paradox inherent in that state of affairs. This is by no means a complaint on my part: despite having at least

tried to rationalize the act of flight on physical grounds, I never cease to marvel that any animal could ever acquire the ability to get off the ground.

I think one of the reasons why this is such a puzzle is that there is nothing in our own experience as human beings that really enables us to get to physical grips with the act of flying. For example, we can readily appreciate how animals run, leap or swim because at one time or another in our lives we all engage in these activities. Even if we were asked to empathize with a tunnelling earthworm, a burrowing jerboa or a slithering reptile I think we would only demur from the task if we had completely forgotten what it is like to be a baby or small child wriggling under the bedclothes.

But for most of us there is nothing that we have ever done with our own bodies that comes remotely close to the act of flying. Among human activities, the pole-vault is the only event that comes to mind – involving the use of sheer muscle power to launch one's body up into the air. Few readers will ever have engaged in this sport; that is a pity, because only then will you experience at first hand the incredible effort that is needed to keep your body airborne for even one or two seconds, using your own resources. Animal flight may sometimes appear effortless looked at from the outside, but most of the time it is very hard work indeed!

It is only natural that when we try to understand animal flight we are drawn into comparisons with man-made aircraft. This is fine as long as we remember that there is one enormous difference between aeroplanes and flying animals. All the work of a modern jet aircraft is done by the engine installed in its fuselage – the wings do no real work at all. In contrast, the flapping wings of an animal do all the work, driving the body forward through the air and at the same time producing the lift to keep the animal at a steady altitude above the ground.

At the most fundamental level, the interaction between the surface of the wing and the air in contact with it, all wings, whether they are moving or fixed, exploit the same physical laws. The crucial property of air that enables a wing to create forces from it is that, although it is invisible, it has weight. We feel its weight when the wind blows, and it is also responsible for the atmospheric pressure around us. Each time we take a breath we draw in about half a gramme of air. Air is a fluid medium, and flying animals use exactly the same principle as swimming animals to propel themselves through it: in order to make your body move through the medium, you must at the same time move the medium. This is why flying and swimming

animals are uniquely different from all others. Animals living on the ground move by levering their bodies against an immovable medium, and in order to do this without slipping they rely on friction.

The insect as a propelled aircraft

Flying and swimming animals are making use of Newton's Second Law: every action has an equal and opposite reaction. In a nutshell this means that the wing hits the air, accelerates the air particles, and in return experiences a 'back force' from the air. We can make a simple analogy with a bat hitting a ball. After being hit, the ball speeds off at right-angles to the bat, but at the same time the hand of the person holding the bat experiences a momentary force in the opposite direction. Agreed, this seems a long way from real flying!

But suppose you are an astronaut floating weightless in a space ship but nevertheless eager to maintain your golf handicap. The ball is stationary before you (it does not require a tee), you finally brace yourself, take a full-blooded swipe right on target and send the ball hurtling off at high speed. But at the same time, assuming that you were able in some way to keep track of your own centre of gravity, you would find that you yourself were moving slowly backwards in the opposite direction to the ball. You have given the ball 'action' and are now experiencing a 'reaction'. This is still not flying, but it is getting close!

We can think of the air as being made up of countless tiny particles each of which, like the golfball in the spaceship, has weight. Each time a flying animal's wings beat against the air, the particles are made to accelerate away from the wing and the wing in turn experiences a lifting force that counters the weight of the body. This is why there could never be a flying animal (bird, bat or insect) that did not leave behind it a wake of moving medium, any more than a propelled ship could move forward without leaving a wake behind its stern. The energy in the wake is an historical record of the effort the wings have made to keep the body moving forwards in level flight.

Few people are ever likely to find themselves in circumstances where they can test out the 'golfer in the spaceship' analogy of flight, but it is just possible to construct a model rather closer to home. Suppose we build a trolley supported on four virtually frictionless wheels and run it on the flattest, smoothest surface available – say a huge pane of plate glass. The trolley must be large enough to accommodate one person plus a large stack of metal 1kg weights, as depicted in Figure 18. There are no other props.

We now invent a game called 'Move the trolley and yourself without touching the ground'. To play this game you must be standing (or seated) on the trolley. Readers who have followed the weightless golfer analogy will not hesitate to climb on to the trolley, grasp the weights and enthusiastically hurl a succession of them out of the back as quickly as possible. Each time the hand accelerates the weight backwards from the vehicle a force will be transmitted down through the arm, body and legs, imparting a small amount of forward momentum to the vehicle. The faster the weights are thrown, the more likely it is that the trolley will overcome the small amount of friction in its wheels and pick up speed. We now have an automobile that is driven by purely inertial forces, and are actually well on our way to reinventing the propelled aircraft.

The trouble with the 'inertia-mobile' is that it soon runs out of weights to produce the inertial forces. However, at this stage it seems a pity to abandon the principle, so why not try and use the air around us? After all, there is an endless supply of it.

As a second experiment we install on the rear of the trolley a very large fan, which can be cranked by hand through a set of gears. The fan sucks air particles in from the front and expels them at greatly increased velocity to the rear. Each air particle that has crossed through the fan blades must therefore have been accelerated, imparting a reactive force to the blades, down through the gear linkages and on to the trolley.

Now comes the third and most ambitious experiment: to convert the fan-driven trolley into an aircraft. In theory all that we need to do is equip the trolley with a pair of fixed wings having the appropriate camber and angle of attack. Then, as the trolley gains speed, the airflow around the wings will begin to generate lift and the trolley will rise from the ground.

In practice, of course, the entire machine will have to be scrapped and rebuilt, using the lightest materials available that will be able to take the stresses. Also, we are not just building an aeroplane; this aeroplane must be powered by the muscles of a single person. The idea of a hand-cranked fan will

How to induce forward motion in a machine by ejecting mass from behind

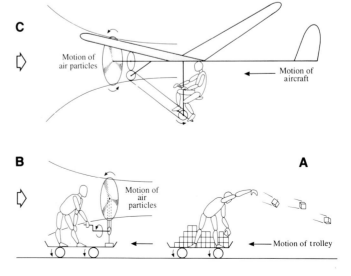

Figure 18. The fundamental principle of flight is the same as that governing all motion: Newton's Second Law, which states that 'every action has an equal and opposite reaction'. 'Action' here means 'force'. The lifting force on a wing is a reaction from the air that has been accelerated downwards and behind the wing. In order to understand this, it helps to think of the air as being made up of tiny particles each having a finite mass. A man standing on a trolley can induce forward motion by throwing weights from behind, as seen in **A**. The same objective could be achieved by using a fan to accelerate a jet of air from behind, as in **B**. Fitting such a fan to a light aircraft frame provides a basis for man-powered 'flight', as shown in **C**. A fuller explanation is given in the text.

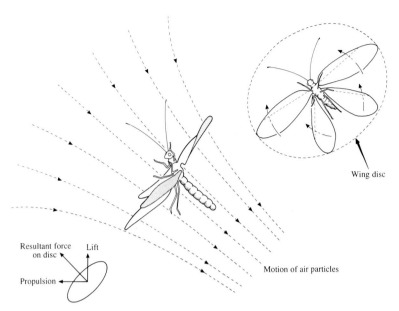

Wing disc

Resultant force
on disc

Lift

Propulsion

Motion of air particles

Figure 19. Like a propeller or the rotor blades of a helicopter, the beating wings of an insect produce a current of air from in front and expel it from behind at higher velocity. The acceleration of the air particles through the wings provides the reactive force on the wings that keeps the body aloft. The forces acting on the insect as a result of the fluid motion through the wings can be analysed by substituting the insect's body and wings by an imaginary 'wing disc' enclosed within the wing tip path, as shown in the inset. The wing disc is orientated in the stroke plane of the insect. The force generated by the wings acts at right-angles to the wing disc and can be resolved into a vertical lift component and a horizontal thrust or propulsive component, as shown lower left. When the wing disc is horizontal, as it is in a hovering insect, all the force produced is vertical. When the insect moves forward, the wing disc is tilted forward and both lift and thrust components are produced.

have to be jettisoned; there is simply not enough power available in the arms. But there might just be enough power in the bulk of the legs and buttocks together. The fan will have to be driven through a set of bicycle gears.

This series of hypothetical arguments may seem a little far-fetched until we realize that man-powered level flight in an aircraft has already been achieved, although only recently. It requires every ounce of strength of a highly trained individual, and can be sustained at most for a few minutes. This final conquest of the air brings home to us what a monumental achievement the evolution of animal flight has been. But it also highlights a critical point. The key to the origin of flight in animals is not necessarily the evolution of the wing itself but the ability to commit an enormous bulk of muscle, equivalent to as much as half the weight of the entire body, to the task of driving the wing.

An aircraft driven by a propeller provides only a very crude model of animal flight, its principal weakness being that it has fixed wings. On the bonus side, a propeller generates aerodynamic forces in very much the same way as a bird's or insect's wings. Both function by drawing a stream of air from in front and ejecting it behind at greatly increased velocity. The energy contained in the air currents or vortexes being shed from revolving propellers and flapping wings is an indication of how much force the surface of the propeller or wing is in turn receiving from the air.

This idea provides the basis of the so-called momentum disc theory of animal flight. The theory starts by likening the flapping wings to a set of helicopter rotor blades. The tips of the blades trace out a circle as they revolve, similar to the circle traced out by the wing tips of a bird or insect as they move backwards and forwards in the stroke plane. The area circumscribed by the circle is referred to as the wing disc. Flight consists of drawing a current of air into one face of the disc and accelerating it out of the other as a jet. The force on the disc, which is the same as the force produced by the flapping wings, is equivalent to the momentum injected into the jet. The wing disc of a hovering insect is horizontal, so all the force experienced by the disc is upward – in other words, lift. When an insect moves forward the wing disc is tilted forward, so that the force can be resolved into two components, one directed upward and keeping the body aloft (lift), the other directed backwards and driving the body forward (propulsion) (Figure 19).

Wings, wakes and air vortexes

The wing disc model of animal flight is useful because it enables us to see the relationships between air currents and the reactive forces on the wings, without cluttering our minds with the details of how the

73. Viewed from below the body, the wings of an insect give the impression of two pairs of propellers rotating within the same plane. **A** shows a green lacewing, **B** a scorpion fly *Panorpa communis*. In both these insects we know that the fore wings precede the hind wings in their movements, so that if the body is moving forwards their stroke planes cannot coincide geometrically. However, as explained in the text, the movements of the two wing pairs are timed so that the hind wing slipstreams the fore wing. In effect, therefore, both wing pairs are moving in the same dynamic plane and the helicopter blade analogy is acceptable. In this case, in order to model the relationships between the air flow created by the wings and the resultant forces on the wings, it is possible to substitute the insect by an imaginary 'wing disc', equivalent to the circle swept out by the wings during each beat. This device provides the basis of the so-called 'momentum disc' model of insect flight, as discussed in the text and illustrated in Figure 19.

A

B ▶

wings are moving and exactly how the force is being created at the wing surface. The model very elegantly makes the point, which we were struggling to achieve in a much more roundabout way earlier in this chapter, that flying animals gain force by accelerating air into their wake. It is only in relatively recent years that scientists interested in flight have appreciated the importance of the wake as a kind of signature of what the wings are doing to the air to make lift.

Experiments have been designed to visualize the wake by making birds or insects fly through a cloud of harmless dust particles or neutrally buoyant bubbles, which are then photographed using highly specialized techniques. The paths traced out by the particles indicate the currents of air that are generated behind the animal. Such experiments were inspired directly by the momentum jet model and have enormously increased our understanding of flight. But they have also shown up the painful inadequacies of the model and forced us to think more realistically about the way that air behaves when it comes into contact with a flapping wing. The momentum disc model has served its purpose and led to a much better model which

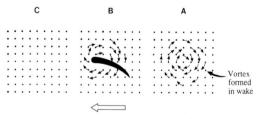

Movement of aerofoil

Figure 20. Imagine that you are a stationary observer and that the wing of an aircraft is moving horizontally across your field of view from right to left. As it moves, the wing will disturb the air and leave behind it a trail of circulating air particles. Let us see what happens to the air in three different fields of the forward path of the wing, numbered **A**, **B** and **C** from right to left. Field **C** has not yet been disturbed by the wing. The wing has reached field **B** and, owing to its positive angle of attack, the lower surface pushes the air downwards and forwards. But since air is a fluid, particles must at the same time circulate on to the upper surface of the wing to maintain continuity. The wing cannot carry such a 'bound' circulation with it from one field to the next but leaves the disturbance behind in its wake as a vortex, as in **A**. A trail of such vortexes forms as the wing moves forward.

takes account of the fact that air is a fluid, so that when a wing strikes it, it will not simply move in a straight line. Instead it will recirculate around the wing as a vortex.

The vortex theory of animal flight is quite revolutionary and has brought the subject into step with the latest aerodynamic ideas. It allows us to see much more clearly what is happening to the air as it flows over and away from the wing. We are also beginning to understand how the shape, texture and elasticity of animal wings have been moulded by interaction with the airflow circulating around them.

The word 'circulating' is very important here. When we look at the wake of a flying animal we find that the air is not flowing backwards like a jet, as the momentum disc theory suggests, but like a regular series of tubular vortexes or mini-whirlwinds. The vortex theory tells us how these whirlwinds are formed. As a wing moves through the air it has to accelerate the air to gain force. In our simpler models we suggested that the air was accelerated behind as a jet made up of innumerable air particles travelling in a straight line. The vortex theory reminds us that we need to think harder. Air is a fluid, not a collection of tiny billiard balls, and a surface such as a wing cannot simply make it flow in one direction: it must *recirculate*. This is the basis of lift generation by wings: air is made to circulate around the wing, and after circulation it is cast off behind as a vortex.

Modern techniques have not yet reached the stage where we can actually see the vortexes as they are formed around the wing; we depend mainly on information gained from visualization of the wake. But working forwards, as it were, from the wake towards the surface of the wings that formed it, it is possible to reconstruct the likely course of events leading to vortex formation.

As the wing moves through the air a tubular vortex forms along its whole length, surrounding the wing rather like a Swiss roll with its centre aligned parallel to the long axis of the wing. At any one 'snapshot' moment of time the vortex appears to be bound to the wing, but in fact new lengths of

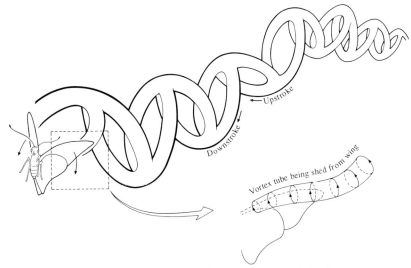

Figure 21. A flying insect leaves behind it a wake, just like the wake of a ship. The wake consists of a chain of linked vortex rings traced out by the wing tips. The rings are tilted forward during the upstroke and backward during the downstroke, and successive rings are linked at the stroke extremes. As the inset shows, the vortexes are formed by air circulating under pressure from the lower surface of the wing to the upper surface, around the leading edge. Vortex tubes formed in this way along the leading edge become 'shed' from the wing tips and eventually coalesce to form the vortex rings. The strength of air circulation within the vortex tubes is proportional to the speed of movement of the wing through the air. The stronger the circulation of air in the vortexes, the greater the reactive forces of lift and propulsion induced on the wings.

point where two friends are waiting, each an arm's length away from the middle of the road. As you pass, each friend grasps the cuff of one of your sleeves and begins to walk in the direction from which you have come. You continue walking forwards and the sleeves of your jumper start to roll endlessly along your arms, over your hands and into the two parallel streamers being pulled out by your friends. The sleeve is the tubular vortex being continuously formed by the flying animal's wing. As each new section of sleeve moves along the arm it represents the bound part of the vortex. As it slips over the hand downstream, it represents the shed part of the vortex.

However this model is incorrect in one important respect: the wings of a flying animal are not fixed but move up and down. The tubular vortex shed from the tip of each wing follows the wing tip path. The result is that the vortex wake is not in the form of two parallel lines, as the simple model above predicts, but in a series of linked 'smoke' rings, as shown in Figure 21.

The importance of a scientific discovery lies not only in the new information that it brings to light but also in the fresh perspectives that it offers on previously unexplained events. For instance, the vortex theory of animal flight may explain why the front and hind wings are firmly coupled in some insects but conspicuously uncoupled in others.

Suppose we take two insects, both of which have two pairs of wings strongly coupled together in their movements. The insects beat the wings at exactly the same rate but differ in that one of the insects has a forward air speed much greater than that of the other. (For the purposes of the argument it doesn't matter why the air speeds are different.)

We now need to look closely at the airflow in the immediate vicinity of the wing tips, and it will help to refer to Figure 23. Remember that as the wing tips move through the air they leave behind them a tubular vortex.

Consider first the faster-flying insect. As Figure 23 shows, the body of this insect

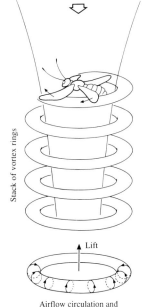

Airflow towards wing disc

Stack of vortex rings

Lift

Airflow circulation and force on vortex ring

vortex tube are being formed continuously. Each section of newly formed vortex moves steadily outwards towards the wing tip, from where it is shed into the wake.

The situation can perhaps be pictured more clearly if we use our arms as wings, as we have done in previous chapters. Imagine you are walking up the middle of a straight road, arms stretched out horizontally to the side. You are wearing a jumper with infinitely extensible sleeves. You reach a

Figure 22. A hovering insect beats its wings in an almost horizontal stroke plane. Each upward or downward stroke of the wings generates a vortex ring which is thrown down below the body. Since the insect is hovering, and has no forward movement, the only aerodynamic force is the lifting force, which is equal to the weight of the insect. This force is produced by the wings but only at the expense of a large amount of energy that must be injected into the air in the form of vortex rings.

moves through a large horizontal distance for each stroke of its wings, so that the vortex tubes are drawn out into a series of long, shallow ripples. Concentrate now on the tips of the front and hind wings of each side. Although the tips are separated slightly, the distance between them is so small compared to the wavelength of the vortex 'ripple' that in effect the hind wing tip moves exactly in the wake of the fore wing tip. So the hind wing tip sheds its vortex into the vortex already coming from the front wing tip and the two fuse smoothly and without interference.

Now look at the slow-flying insect. For each beat of the wings the body now moves forward only a short distance. The spacing between the fore and hind wing tips is now significant compared to the wavelength of

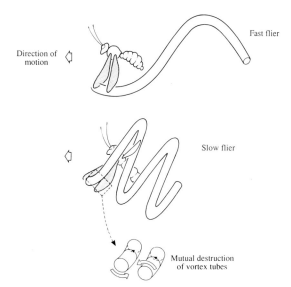

Direction of motion

Fast flier

Slow flier

Mutual destruction of vortex tubes

Figure 23. The fact that the beating wings of an insect leave behind them a vortex tube may help to explain why in many species the fore and hind wings need to beat out of phase. In a fast-flying four-winged insect the fore and hind wings must be tightly coupled so that the vortex shed by the hind wing tip does not interfere with that shed by the fore wing tip. In contrast, in a slow-flying insect the vortex tubes shed by the fore and hind wing tips will not coincide but will interfere, if the wings are tightly coupled. This interference of the air circulations will reduce the effectiveness of the wings. In the example of the slow flier, the hind wing would need to be positioned at the point shown (unshaded wing) in order for the tips of both wings to follow the same path. This means that the movement of the hind wing should be delayed with respect to that of the fore wing by just over half a complete cycle.

the vortexes. This means that the separate tips shed their vortex tubes independently and, instead of fusing and reinforcing one another, they interfere with one another. Inevitably the aerodynamic force generated by the wings, which depends on the strength of the vortexes shed from the wings, will be lessened by this interference.

Of course these are hypothetical insects, but Figure 23 also shows how a real insect flying slowly through the air can avoid mutual annihilation of the fore and hind wing vortex tubes. The solution is to adjust the timing of the beating of the hind wing so that it lags behind that of the fore wing by an amount just sufficient to make the two wing tip paths coincide exactly. The hind wing tip will then 'slipstream' the fore wing tip.

But you will appreciate that this freedom to alter the relative timing of the beating of the two wings depends on their being able to move completely independently; hence the need to uncouple the wings. I cannot claim that the vortex theory provides a complete explanation of the wing coupling question, but it is consistent with field observations: many relatively slow-flying insects such as lacewings, ant-lions, scorpion flies, snake flies, bush-crickets, grasshoppers and mantids possess fore and hind wings which are only loosely coupled and move strongly out of phase with one another.

The flight of dragonflies

As with every generalization there are exceptions: dragonflies, for instance, are fast, powerful fliers but have completely uncoupled wings that beat strongly out of phase. But if you watch a 'hawker' such as one of the *Aeshna* species patrolling its streamside territory you will see that, between high-speed darts, it too is capable of carefully inching its way forward between the wind-blown reeds; and it is in these circumstances that the vortex argument again applies.

Time spent looking more closely at the flight of dragonflies and their sisters, the damselflies will be repaid. Few of us could fail to have our spirits raised just a little by the sight of their netted wings trembling

A **B**

74. Dragonflies are extremely versatile fliers, capable of adjusting their wing beat pattern to suit widely different manoeuvres. In **A,** this *Sympetrum* is beating the wings in a counterstroking mode and the fore and hind pairs are out of phase by about half a cycle. This type of stroking is typical of slow forward and hovering flight. During 'darts', as in **B,** the wings are moved together in 'parallel-stroking'. In this photograph, both wing pairs have just reached the bottom of the downstroke.

(sometimes quite noisily!) in the sky. As I write, it is September, and the hedgerows of Cambridgeshire are alive with the dragonflies *Sympetrum*, *Aeshna cyanea* and, rather less commonly, *Aeshna grandis*. At times, each step that you take as you walk through the fields sends up a small cloud of Sympetrums from the dying thistle heads and brittle hogweed stems. Even though blazing stubble fields, lit by assiduous fenland farmers, have transformed the landscape into a Napoleonic battlefield, the throng of dragonflies seems unperturbed. They simply fall back from one hedgerow to the next as the line of fire approaches. More and more dragonflies become concentrated along fewer and fewer hedgerows: after all, there is little point in returning once the fire has been extinguished.

Most people would agree that dragonflies, although closely related to damselflies, seem much more agile and powerful fliers, and this impression is confirmed by closer inspection. Photographs of damselflies in

flight often show the wings held in a characteristic 'windmill' configuration. This is because the fore and hind wings are moved out of phase by a full half stroke, a type of flight referred to as counterstroking. Counterstroking is well suited to the needs of slow-flying insects such as damselflies, lacewings and ant-lions because, as we saw earlier, it harmonizes the wakes being shed from the wings. But it also produces a more uniform flight, a 'smoother' ride, because any inequalities in lift production between the upstroke and the downstroke of each wing pair are exactly cancelled.

So the flight of damselflies is efficient, but they are slow and have relatively little performance in reserve. Their main advantage over dragonflies is that they are able to vary the angle of the stroke plane and beat their wings through a greater amplitude. For example, the wings are able to move backwards and forwards absolutely horizontally, almost like helicopter blades – something that a dragonfly cannot do. Thus, although their flight is relatively weak, damselflies can hover without difficulty.

Some readers will be familiar with the unusual meticulousness with which damselflies search out a spot on which to alight, weaving slowly in and out of the grass stems. Heaven knows what finally prompts them to choose one grass stem in preference to another looking perfectly identical, but the whole time-consuming manoeuvre is only made possible by this ability to twist the wing bases so that they move horizontal to the ground.

Dragonflies display a much greater variety of stroke pattern. The frequency, amplitude and phase of the wing beat can all be varied to produce a broad spectrum of flight velocity, acceleration and manoeuvres. Most importantly, they are not confined to a counterstroke mode of wing beat. The phase relationships between the fore and hind wings can be altered over the full range from counterstroke to parallel stroke, when the wings are beating absolutely together. Changes from one mode to the other can be accomplished within the 'flick of a wing'.

Parallel stroking is suited to fast, darting flight. The fore and hind wing tips move together so that, during high-speed flight, the shed vortexes reinforce one another. But it can also produce a rougher ride because any differences in aerodynamic performance between the upstroke and the downstroke are not cancelled, as they are in the counterstroking mode, but enhanced.

Drag forces on the wing

Various different forces act on the wing as it moves through the air. Briefly these are the weight of the air, the viscous 'drag' of the air and the weight of the wing itself. We have already seen that the weight of the air is in fact the only thing that makes flight possible at all. At the same time, since the wing must accelerate this mass of air in order to produce the lift, the air effectively imposes a load on the wings and hence on the wing muscles. This load induced on the moving wing by the weight of the air is known technically as the induced drag. This term distinguishes it from the viscous drag, the second of the resistance forces, which is due to friction exerted on the moving wing surfaces by the viscosity of the air. Almost all the friction occurs within the very narrow zone of air nearest the wing surface (the boundary layer), measuring only a fraction of a millimetre in depth.

In engineering situations friction is usually thought of as a source of wasted energy, and so it is in the case of a flying animal. Any moving surface presented to the air, including the head, body, wings and legs, will create friction, and many insects and birds have a streamlined profile in order to reduce frictional effects. But friction also has its uses. Running and walking animals rely on friction to gain purchase with the ground as they move, whilst in flying animals frictional forces within the boundary layer promote smooth or laminar airflow over the surface of the wing. Any modification of the wing surface which increases air resistance within the boundary layer will therefore promote laminar flow and prevent the formation of turbulent eddies. This is why the surface of insect wings is often dotted with microscopic hairs or microtrichia, and the scales on the wings of butterflies probably serve the same purpose.

The third element in the catalogue of resistance forces is the weight of the wing itself. We saw in Chapter 4 that the effective mass of even a tiny lightweight wing in-

75. At the microscopic level the surface of a wing is anything but smooth. Many wings are clothed in minute hairs or microtrichia measuring less than 1/10 mm in height. The microtrichia increase the viscous drag of the surface, helping to maintain 'laminar' flow conditions. Butterfly scales probably serve a similar aerodynamic role.

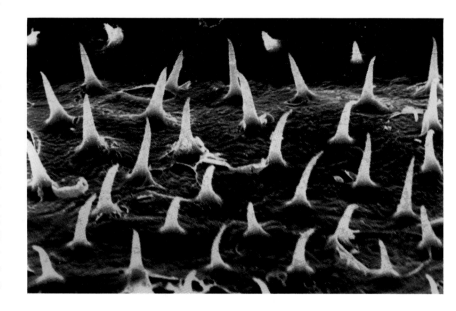

76. The wing cases of the beetles *Lagria hirta* (**A**) and *Agapanthea* (**B**) are covered in long hairs or macrotrichia which extend beyond the boundary layer of the air flowing over the wings. Such hairs would hamper the smooth flow of air over a moving wing, but since the wing cases of beetles play no part in flight they do not encounter this problem.

creases as soon as it is vibrated, and this immediately imposes an additional burden on the wing muscles.

From this brief review it can be appreciated that wing design in insects must be based on a delicate equation of forces. The wing must be light enough to reduce the inertial load on the muscles to tolerable levels, but also substantial enough to support the weight of the body and withstand aerodynamic forces. At the same time, choice of materials is critical: the wing needs

structural strength, but it must also be able to bend. Its surface needs to be smooth in order to allow the air to glide across without resistance – yet not perfectly smooth, otherwise it will not be able to form a boundary layer which clings to the surface. Whenever we look closely at a wing we must bear these points in mind, but there are many other architectural features in its design which remain a complete mystery. A full account of the design features of even the simplest-looking wing is probably still decades away.

77. Butterflies are amongst the most versatile of insect fliers. Their large wings beat slowly and silently, concealing the use of ingenious techniques for extracting forces out of the air. One of these methods involves peeling the wings apart during the downstroke, as we see in this rear view of a large white *Pieris brassicae.*

· 7 ·

GALLEONS OF THE BREEZE

If mayflies are the skipping ballerinas of the air, and dragonflies are the combat helicopters, we can surely liken butterflies to galleons: stately at rest, but capable of an impressive turn of speed. Indeed, like ships, butterflies seem to enjoy a good breeze. On windy days, when other insects are grimly hanging on to the swaying branches and grass stems, butterflies are meeting the challenge head-on in their eager search for nectar, a mate or a suitable place to lay their eggs. Only when the sun is erased by the clouds, or the wind becomes too cold or too strong, will they retreat reluctantly to the ground. In the heady days of summer one gains the feeling that night-time inactivity is an enforced penance for these insects, so driven are they by the need to be airborne.

Such mastery on the wing rests on an ability to react swiftly to buffeting air currents of the kind that would swamp other, less capable, fliers. The size and frequency of the wing beat, the angle of the stroke plan and the tilt of the body can all be shifted rapidly as the occasion demands, and complex twisting and turning manoeuvres can be expedited within a single stroke of the wings. Most insects, except dragonflies and the extremely agile Diptera, would probably need a dozen or more wing beats to achieve the same result.

As we saw in Chapter 4, high-speed photographs surprise us with the amount of flexural distortion that they show taking place in the wings during flight. In the case of butterflies, the waves passing through the wings often give the impression of a moving curtain: one can almost hear the swish of the fabric as one examines the pictures. The rippling appearance of these wings belies their strength. Wing peeling contributes to the remarkable vertical take-off abilities of butterflies, as mentioned in Chapter 3.

Curiously enough, the moving curtain effect of butterfly wings which specialized photographic techniques are beginning to reveal appears to have been known to ancient Japanese calligraphers, to judge from some of their exquisite drawings of butterflies in flight. The wings of a dead butterfly are rigid, a world apart from the living, moving thing. The inspiration for at least some of these drawings must have come from careful observation of the motion of the wings in living butterflies. Perhaps it is possible to train the eye to quicken its powers of image discrimination so that what registers as a blur to most people unfolds as a distinct series of shape changes in the eyes of an expert. The motives of the Chinese calligraphers were not scientific, but artistic. Presumably they were interested in the image, rather than the phenomenon.

Butterflies have an irrational effect on human beings. People who would shriek at the sight of a cockroach, or blithely crush an earwig or beetle underfoot, become almost reverential towards butterflies. We all do it. The love of butterflies is almost entirely due to their decorative appearance; in fact it is partly because so many of them were worshipped as ornaments that so many species have been driven to extinction. Or, more precisely, collected to extinction.

Fortunately nowadays there is a more enlightened attitude to wild animals in general, and to butterflies in particular. One trusts that butterflies are admired for what they are, what they do, and how they do it; and all three of these qualities are snuffed out the moment we kill them and display them in a glass case. Nevertheless it is still possible to encounter serious European lepidopterists in the field casually crushing between their fingers specimens of any species which they consider too 'abundant' for the good of the rest of the butterfly community. To control a species because it poses a serious threat to the food supplies of man or other animals strikes me as perfect sense; culling it in the name of some unproven notion of natural balance persuades me of nothing except the staggering arrogance of certain conservationists.

Figure 24. Sequence of wing movements during the stroke cycle of a butterfly, reconstructed from original photographs. The sequence begins at the lower left and ends at the upper right. Further details are given in the text.

Wing peeling as a way of making lift

The recognition that butterflies do something rather special with their wings was originally due to Torkel Weis-Fogh, former

Professor of Zoology at Cambridge University. While studying the flight mechanics of the green-veined white *Pieris napi* and large white *P. brassicae* butterflies he worked out that, if their wings had behaved like conventional fixed aerofoils obeying the 'steady-state' laws of aerodynamics, they could not possibly have supported the body in the air. They were the wrong shape and did not beat fast enough. Weis-Fogh deduced that these clever insects were generating extra lift by a mechanism unknown to aerodynamicists but which he had already identified in a tiny parasitic wasp called *Encarsia formosa*.

This wasp was a living refutation of the idea that insects fly like aeroplanes, since it was observed to take off from the ground even before the wings had made a stroke! It happened like this: when *Encarsia* is about to take off it raises both wing pairs above its body until they are in contact back-to-back. The leading edges of the front pair of wings are now rotated outwards, so that a wedge-shaped gap begins to form between the wings of each side. As it is twisting out the leading edges, the wasp is careful to make sure that the trailing edges of the hind wings remain in contact; otherwise the gap would open behind as well as in front. As the gap widens a vacuum is created between the wings and air circulates around the leading edges into the gap; the effect is that the wings experience a lifting force. In Chapter 6 it was explained that the condition for a wing to produce lift is that air circulates around it in the form of a vortex. *Encarsia* makes this happen even before the wings as a whole have separated and begun their descent.

Readers will recognize the similarities between the clap and fling mechanism of *Encarsia* and the 'peel' practised by butterflies and described in Chapter 3. Butterflies have highly flexible wings which are perfectly adapted for the peeling mechanism. You will recall that, as the wings separate at the beginning of the peeling process, air becomes drawn into the gap between the leading edges. But there is also a tendency for air to be drawn in from behind, around the trailing edges. This would completely

undermine the lift-generating process, because the air circulation coming in from behind would annihilate that coming in from in front. The highly flexible expanded anal lobes of the hind wings prevent this happening because they 'stick' together until the very last moment of the peeling process, acting as a valve against the retrograde flow. This sequence of events can readily be understood by examining photographs of butterfly wings in various stages of the peel.

Some butterflies have developed a sophisticated variant of the peel which they use during the upstroke, but it can only be seen by very careful 'photographic dissection' of the wing movements right at the start of this phase of the cycle. Photographically speaking, this is not an easy task to perform, because it involves documenting movements that are taking place directly beneath the body. For obvious reasons it is much easier to photograph a freely flying insect from the side or even from above the body. To understand the process of 'funnel formation', as this novel type of peeling will be described, we need to focus on the movements of the wings just after they have momentarily come to rest at the end of the downstroke. For an instant they are poised to begin the upstroke, the wing tips almost but not quite touching one another in the mid-line directly below the body. As the wings draw apart, it is the fore wing that leads the movement. At the same time the leading edge of the fore wing begins to roll back or supinate. At this stage the effect is virtually the mirror image of the peeling process that occurs above the body at the start of the downstroke: the same steadily growing wedge-shaped gap between the wings, bordered in front by the leading edges of the fore wings, sealed behind by the apposed hind wings.

But as the gap grows in size, the shape changes taking place in the wing become more complicated. In Chapter 4 it was explained that wings often become strongly arched downwards at the start of the upstroke. This also happens in butterfly wings. The result is that we now have two flexural forces acting simultaneously on the wings. One acts along the chord of the wings from the leading edge of the fore wing to the trailing edge of the hind wing: this is the natural consequence of the peeling process. The other acts at right-angles to this along the span of the wings and is the downward flexural force just alluded to. Fortunately, the

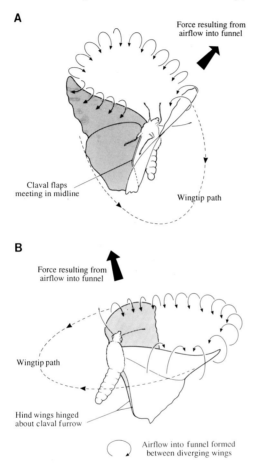

Figure 25. These drawings (taken directly from original photographs) show views of the body of a butterfly from below (**A**) and above (**B**) just after the wings have begun their upstroke movement. At the bottom of the immediately preceding downstroke the wing tips will have been apposed together. Now, as the upstroke begins, the fore wings move in advance of the hind wings. The leading edges of the fore wings also become strongly flexed downwards. The overall result is that early in the upstroke the wings of each side of the body enclose between them a funnel-shaped cavity, the mouth of which is enclosed by the curved leading edges of the fore wings, and the narrow throat of which is formed by the closely apposed trailing edges of the hind wings. As the wings draw apart air is sucked over the leading edge into the funnel, creating a force which accelerates the body upwards. **B** shows how the claval flaps of the hind wings help in funnel formation. The flaps seal the throat of the funnel against any leakage of air from behind and below, since leakage of this kind would interfere with the smooth flow of air into the mouth.

butterfly wing is so flexible that it readily moulds itself to both these forces even though they are pulling in different directions. The result is that the wings distort into the shape of a vase or funnel, the leading edges forming the mouth, the trailing edges forming the tapered body and throat.

The funnel works in the same way as the peel, only it is probably more efficient. As long as the funnel is enlarging, air will circulate into its mouth and the sealed hind wings will make sure that this one-way flow is least disrupted by currents drawn in from behind. By this stage the body of the butterfly has been pitched 'nose-up', as we saw in Chapter 3. Since the main axis of the funnel is more or less aligned with the body axis, as photographs 85A, 85B and 86A show, the main force caused by the air being sucked into the funnel is directed vertically upwards. Funnel formation seems to be an important part of the vertical take-off manoeuvre.

The process of funnel formation has deliberately been described as though it occurred very gradually, but in reality the whole event lasts only a few hundredths of a second. Brevity indeed is the essence of the process; the funnel can only work because it is formed quickly. It can no more work slowly than a jet turbine could work by slowly exhausting gas from behind.

And how is the funnel more efficient than the peel? This is where downward flexure of the wings plays its role. When the wings arch downwards they form an effective seal around the boundary of the funnel, allowing the air to flow into the funnel only via the mouth. Upward flexure of the wing would benefit the process of peeling to the same degree but, as we saw earlier, wings are designed to flex downwards, not upwards.

Obviously the funnel effect can only last until the point where the wings have separated to a certain extent. Beyond this point air leaks in through the wing tips and the effect rapidly disappears. But by this time the funnel has served its purpose by tiding the wings over a period where they are not moving fast enough to create lift by the conventional aerodynamic mechanism.

78. The wings of butterflies often clap together above the body at the end of the upstroke in preparation for the peeling process that occurs during the early part of the downstroke. This 'clap and peel' mechanism is used particularly during take-off and climbing flight. These photographs illustrate various stages of wing clap in different species. **A**, dark green fritillary *Mesoacidalia aglaja*. **B,** Queen of Spain fritillary *Issoria lathonia*. **C,** small tortoiseshell *Aglais urticae*.

B

A

C ▶

79. Examples of wing clap in: **A**, scarce swallowtail *Iphiclides podalirius*; **B,** green-veined white *Pieris napi* and **C**, orange tip *Anthocaris cardamines*.

A

B

C

D

E

F

80. These rear views of Lepidoptera in flight illustrate various stages of the hind wing peeling process during the initial stages of the downstroke. (**A**) lilac beauty moth *Apeira syringaria*. (**B** and **C**) red underwing moth *Catocala nupta*. (**D**) meadow brown *Maniola jurtina*. (**E**) unidentified fritillary. (**F**) large emerald moth *Geometra papilionaria*.

A

81. Front views of meadow brown *Maniola jurtina* (**A**), woodland grayling *Hipparchia fagi* (**B**) and dark green fritillary *Mesoacidalia aglaja* (**C**) butterflies which have just completed the peeling phase of the downstroke. Viewed from below, we see how in **A** and **C** the large claval lobes of the hind wing hug the abdomen and effectively seal the space between the upper and lower wing surfaces.

B

C ▶

A

B ▶

C

82. In these photographs the wings have just reached the lowest point in the downstroke. Although the wing tips often make contact at the end of the upstroke, as shown in photograph sequence 78, full contact between the wing tips is rarely seen at the end of the downstroke. (**A**), clouded yellow *Colias crocea*. (**B**) green-veined white *Pieris napi*, (**C**) tiger *Danaus*. (**D**) peacock *Inachis io*. (**E**), Queen of Spain fritillary *Issoria lathonia*.

E

D

83. These rear views of flying butterflies show the wings at a similar stage of the stroke to those shown in photograph sequence 82, but we can see the infolding of the claval lobes of the hind wing. (**A**), small tortoiseshell *Aglais urticae*. (**B**), dark green fritillary *Mesoacidalia aglaja*. (**C**), copper *Heodes virgaureae*. (**D**), black-veined white *Aporia crataegi*. (**E**), red admiral *Vanessa atalanta*.

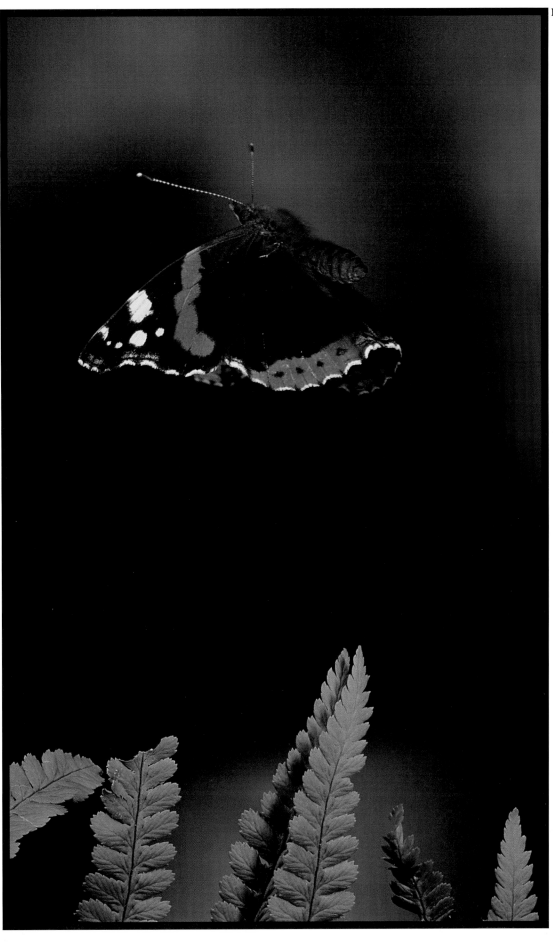

Butterflies have probably devised many other ways of defying these laws of 'steady state' aerodynamics, but which have not yet been identified. These 'unsteady' mechanisms of lift generation depend on the creation of local transient air circulations around the wing, such as the airflow into the mouth of the funnel. There is barely an instant in the flight cycle of a butterfly when its wings are not altering their shape, and helping to create these local circulations. This is why it is no more appropriate to compare a butterfly's wings with the fixed wings of an aeroplane than it is to compare the heaving surface of the ocean with the stillness of a village duckpond.

The wings as 'flap valves'

All that we have seen so far about butterfly wings confirms the importance of the element of elasticity in their design. Neither the peel nor the funnel could operate without it. Elasticity is a general property of insect wings, and butterflies exploit its potential to the limit with the help of another innovation in the form of an enormous expansion of the wing area.

Perhaps the most characteristic feature of butterfly wings is the degree of enlargement of the hind wing, and particularly of the so-called claval lobes which form the inner part of the wing hugging the sides of the abdomen. These lobes are divided off from the main part of the wing by a flexure line, the claval furrow. We saw in Chapter 4 that the claval furrow is very important in the regulation of wing shape. More than any other feature in the butterfly wing, it is the claval lobes that make possible the phenomenon of funnel formation.

We can see this by looking closely at the behaviour of the wing in the region of the claval furrow during flight. It is noticeable that throughout the wing cycle the claval lobes remain stationary. This is because the main part of the hind wing hinges its movement upon the claval furrow. If we observe the wings from a viewpoint above the insect's body, just after they have reached the bottom of the downstroke, we see that the hind wings are folded along the claval

furrow, and the claval lobes are in contact with the sides of the abdomen (see photographs 82E, 83B, 83E and 84A). If we now observe the same stage from a viewpoint directly below the body, we see the claval lobes meeting in the mid-line and completely obscuring the abdomen from view. It looks as though the butterfly is using the claval lobes as a seal to prevent any airflow around the abdomen between the upper and lower surfaces of the wings.

What would be the purpose of such a seal? To answer this question, let us go back to a slightly earlier part of the stroke cycle. If we again concentrate our attention on the upper surface of the insect we see that during the downstroke the abdomen is neatly tucked between the claval lobes of the hind wing. But just as the upstroke begins, the insect seems suddenly to 'arch its back', pulling the abdomen clear from the cleft between the lobes. These movements can be seen in photographs 82A, 82C, 83C and 83D.

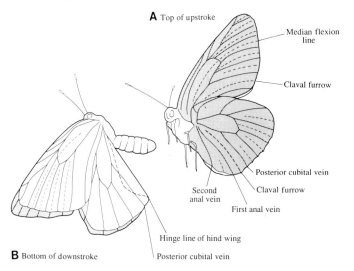

A Top of upstroke

Median flexion line

Claval furrow

Posterior cubital vein

Claval furrow

Second anal vein

First anal vein

Hinge line of hind wing

Posterior cubital vein

B Bottom of downstroke

Figure 26. These drawings of the shape of a butterfly's wings positioned at the top and bottom of the stroke illustrate how the hind wings hinge their motion upon the claval furrow. The species is the black-veined white *Aporia crataegi*, whose clearly delineated venation provides easy references for working out shape changes (see photographs 88A and B). In **A** the entire wing surface is seen from below; note the location of the claval furrow between the posterior cubital vein and the first anal vein. In **B** it can be seen that, in order to achieve its shape at the end of the downstroke, the wing must have folded along the claval furrow, effectively hinging its movement along this flexion line. The dotted line in B indicates the infolded part of the hind wing.

Once the abdomen is out of the way, the left and right claval lobes can now be drawn together tightly, like two folds drawn together by a purse-string. The 'purse-string' is the suction pressure on the lower surfaces of the wing: remember that at this stage the wings are beginning to draw apart and the funnel is beginning to form.

Now the link between funnel formation and the enlargement of the claval lobes should become clear in our minds. Once the claval folds have been drawn together, they effectively seal the apex of the funnel from any ingress of air, from behind or above the abdomen. The mechanism is extraordinarily reminiscent of the way the 'flap valves' of the human heart work. Both mechanisms involve the use of highly mobile flaps of tissue to seal an orifice, and in both cases the valves are regulated by differences in pressure between the inside and the outside of the orifice.

The story of funnel formation in butterfly wings is quite difficult to understand, but it demonstrates the principle that small details make the difference between a mechanism simply working and a mechanism working perfectly. Going no further than the heart valve analogy: if the heart has faulty valves, leakage will occur from the ventricle into the atrium, leading to 'bluing' of the blood. Similarly, if the claval lobes of a butterfly are damaged, the apex of the funnel will not be properly sealed and air will leak into it from behind. Nevertheless, it is not uncommon to see butterflies continuing to fly effectively despite the loss of sizeable fragments of the trailing edges of the wings due to attacks by birds. Presumably these individuals are not flying quite as well as they could and hence are more vulnerable to further attacks.

Wing shape and flight performance

The Lepidoptera is such a varied assembly of insects that it would be surprising if they all flew in exactly the same way. A glance at a manual of butterflies and moths will show a wide range in wing plan form, from the enormous lobed wings of the owl butterfly *Caligo atreus* and the wood nymph *Idea hypermnestra* to the tapering, spear-like fore wings of hawkmoths and the minute, feather-like appendages of the micro-moths, which hardly look like wings at all.

It would be difficult to know where to make a start trying to correlate flight performance and wing architecture in these insects. Even if you restricted your examination to the claval lobes of the hind wings (and you could hardly narrow down your objectives more than that!) you would soon wilt at the thought of the task. For instance, while most of the broad-winged species of European butterflies have a large claval lobe clearly demarcated by a claval furrow, the Papilionidae, which includes many very large tropical species as well as the European Apollo and swallowtail butterflies, have almost non-existent claval lobes. In hawkmoths the hind wing is diminutive and there can be no question of any funneling mechanism involving the claval lobes. Hawkmoths have concentrated on a more conventional design, maximizing the potential of a long, narrow, glider-like wing. Geometrid moths resemble butterflies in general wing shape and in having a well-defined claval lobe in the hind wing, but the lobe seems to behave differently from that of butterflies. High-speed photographs, at least in some species, show that during flight the lobes become folded back over the top of the abdomen, and not under the abdomen as they are in broad-winged butterfly species. It is difficult to see how this arrangement could enhance the process of funnel formation.

So, even in this very restricted part of the wing it may be that we shall have to adjust our thinking to the possibility that different mechanisms may be at work in different groups. Wherever we look, there are new possibilities. Any design engineer aspiring to novel inventions could do worse than spend a few minutes peering down a microscope at one of these wings. After all, the discovery of the peel mechanism of flight in insects prompted engineers towards improvements in the design of turbomachinery!

It will be a daunting task for the future, getting to know our way around the surface of the wing, trying to relate every fold in the landscape to the drainage pattern of the air

A

B

C

D

84. At the beginning of the upstroke, the fore wings move outward in advance of the hind wings. At the same time the leading edge of the fore wing supinates. The triangular, kite-like profile that momentarily results from these movements is particularly evident in **A**. (**A**), scarce swallowtail *Iphiclides podalirius*. (**B**), silver-washed fritillary *Argynnis paphia*. (**C**), clouded buff moth *Diacrisia sannio*. (**D**), large emerald moth *Geometra papilionaria*. (**E**), swallow-tailed moth *Ourapteryx sambucaria*. (**F**), *Dryas julia*.

E

◄ F

A

B

85. Views from directly below the butterfly reveal the striking distortions that take place in the wing at the beginning of the upstroke. These distortions can be resolved into a downward flexure of the leading edge of the fore wing, and a flexure at right-angles to this running across the wings from their leading to their trailing edges. Note how the claval lobes of the hind wings in **A** and **C** have formed a seal around the abdomen, preventing leakage of air between the upper and lower wing surfaces. (**A**), owl *Caligo atreus*. (**B**), red admiral *Vanessa atalanta*. (**C**), scarce swallowtail *Iphiclides podalirius*.

C ▶

A

◀B

86. As the wings continue their ascent towards the halfway point they retain their flexural distortion. (**A**), dark green fritillary *Mesoacidalia aglaja*. (**B**), comma *Polygonia c-album*. (**C**), swallow-tailed moth *Ourapteryx sambucaria*. (**D**), marbled white *Melanargia galathea*.

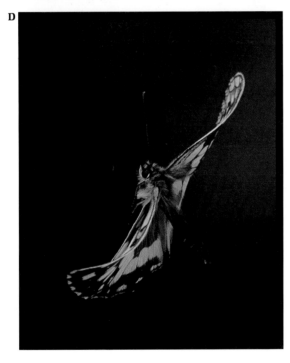

found in the tropics. But general comparisons like this are not really meaningful unless they are accompanied by quantitative measurements. As an additional exercise, it will not be too difficult to take into account the wing loading of different species (the ratio of body weight to wing area) and also the distribution of weight within the wing. These measurements give far more useful information than qualitative comparisons of wing shape.

Indeed, by using concepts such as weight and area distribution patterns, modern biologists interested in flight are trying to quantify wing shape in a way that will make it easier to make precise comparisons between species. To take a simple example: a triangular wing attached to the body by one of its apices concentrates the wing mass away from the body, whilst the same wing

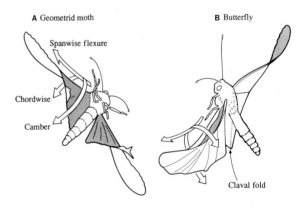

Figure 27. During the upstroke, the wings of a butterfly or a moth experience a combination of aerodynamic and mechanical forces which impose considerable stress on the fabric of the wing. In response to these stresses the wings deform elastically in two main directions. First, the leading edge of the fore wing becomes flexed downwards from its base to its tip and this results in pronounced spanwise camber, that is camber along the length or span of the wing. This type of flexure is due to the lag in the movement of the wing tip compared with the base. The second type of flexure runs across the wings from the leading to the trailing edge, that is across the chord of the wing. This chordwise camber results from the lag in the movement of the hind wing compared with the fore wing. Note how the claval folds of the hind wing of the butterfly form a seal between the upper and lower wing surface, preventing leakage of air around the abdomen. The much smaller claval lobes of the moth hind wing have failed to meet in the middle, possibly resulting in a reduced efficiency of the wings. The undersides of the wings are shaded. The drawings were made directly from photographs 86C and D.

flowing across it. Our present state of knowledge is a long way from this. But in the meantime there is much information to be gained from a more general study of how different wing shapes relate to differences in aerial performance. And in their variety, butterflies and moths lend themselves perfectly to such an undertaking. Amongst butterflies, for example, the short, broad-winged species inhabiting temperate climates have a distinctly different flight habit from the long, narrow-winged types such as the heliconiids and ithomiinids

A

B

87. By the time the wings have ascended to approximately the halfway point in the upstroke, the flexural distortions have almost disappeared. (**A**), swallow-tailed moth *Ourapteryx sambucaria.*(**B**), orange-tip *Anthocaris cardamines.* (**C**), ringlet *Aphantopus hyperantus.*

C ▶

88. A comparison of the different shapes of the hind wing of this black-veined white butterfly *Aporia crataegi* in the fully raised (**A**) and fully lowered (**B**) positions of the stroke reveals how the hind wing hinges its movements along the claval furrow. The furrow can be seen as a line between the second and third veins of the hind wing counting anticlockwise along the trailing edge. These details are made clearer in Figure 26 on page 160.

A

B ▶

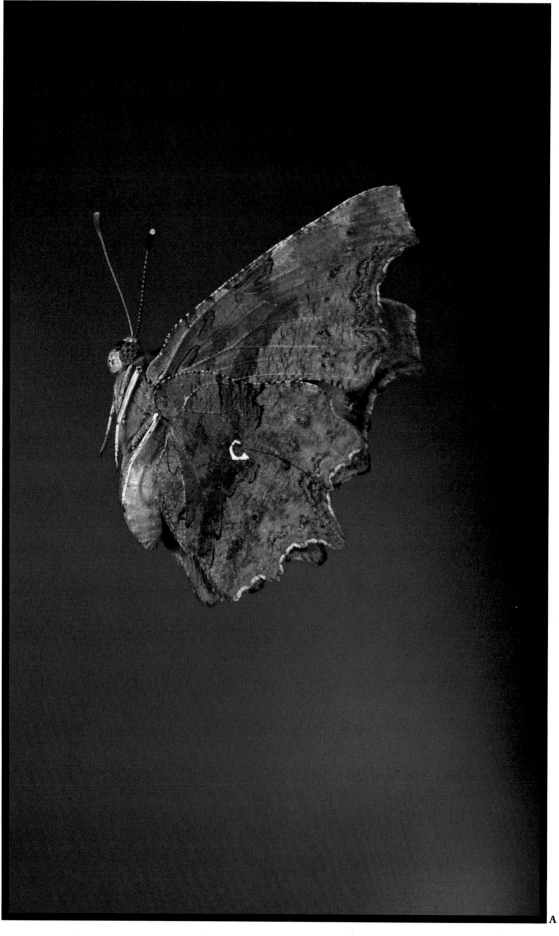

89. This pair of photographs of the comma *Polygonia c-album* shows the wings fully raised (**A**) and fully lowered (**B**) respectively. By carefully comparing the positions of the scalloped edge of the hind wing it will be seen that the main part of the hind wing has hinged downwards along a line coinciding with the claval furrow. Although the claval line of the hind wing cannot be seen as clearly as it appears in the species shown in photograph 88, its position coincides with the straight rear edge of the wing in **B**. Since this is a side view, we cannot see the infolded claval lobes of the hind wing (but see photograph 86B).

A

B ▶

90. The Apollo *Parnassius apollo* is large and heavy-bodied, and experiences great difficulty in taking off from the ground in still air. Its natural habitat is high mountains, where it regularly gains wind assistance. As in most members of the family Papilionidae, the claval lobes of the hind wings are relatively small. The photographs show the wings fully raised (**A**) and fully lowered (**B**) respectively. Despite the absence of sizeable claval lobes, the inner margins of the hind wings still appear to form a seal around the abdomen.

◀**A**

B

91. Careful comparison of these two consecutive stages in the down beat of the red admiral butterfly *Vanessa atalanta* reveal the relationships between the movements of the abdomen and the claval lobes of the hind wings. In **A** the abdomen is exposed between the lobes. Fractionally later, in **B,** the abdomen has been drawn backward, allowing the two lobes to come together.

◄ **A**   **B**

attached by one of its sides draws the weight of the wing inboard. Thus the same wing will impose a completely different inertial load on the muscles when it begins to beat. In the 'tip-heavy' configuration the load is greater because the weight is concentrated on the fastest-moving section of the wing. This configuration also imposes greater stresses on the narrow wing base. On the other hand, having most of the area concentrated near the tip increases the lift production. Putting the weight and area of the wing near the base strengthens the wing attachment and reduces the inertial load, but since the base of the wing does not move up and down with great speed, lift production is less.

It is a question of horses for courses. Some species develop the theme of the broadly attached wing because of the increased strength and manoeuvrability that it confers. Others opt for the more paddle-like configuration because it produces lift at very slow wing beat frequencies, and being able to lower the wing beat frequency in turn places less stress on the narrow wing base.

The very delicate heliconiid butterflies provide an interesting case. Visitors to tropical butterfly houses will be familiar with the fluttering, tantalizing flight of *Heliconia charitonius* (the 'Zebra') and *Dryas julia* (the 'Julia'). The tapering front wings of these species approximate closely to the ideal glider-like shape and are so efficient at producing lift that the insects can afford to beat them only slowly and through small angles. The thorax is slender and capable of housing only a small amount of flight muscle. This means that, although these butterflies are very efficient fliers, they lack power and manoeuvrability. Released into your garden, even assuming that the outside temperature was high enough to prevent them from becoming torpid, they could not possibly cope with the regular wind buffeting that is meat and bread to any of our native broad-winged species.

But the natural home of heliconiids is tropical rainforest, where the air for the most part is relatively still. So we can see that the flight habit of these butterflies is intimately adapted to their environment. Their lack of

rapid, evasive behaviour might, it could be thought, make them easy targets for insectivorous birds – but in many cases chemical defences compensate for this deficiency.

The last group of butterflies that we shall consider, the swallowtails, belong to the opposite end of the flight spectrum from the leisurely heliconiids. Swallowtail flight is altogether far more powerful and agile, and since many species appear as regular items in the diet of birds, this is what you would expect in an insect that frequently has to run for its life. The front wing is very large and pointed, with the weight concentrated near its base. This promotes manoeuvrability without sacrificing lift production. The body is quite stout and muscular, capable of driving the wings rapidly and powerfully through large stroke angles.

In the mountains of southern Europe, the common swallowtail *Papilo machaon* can often be seen beating hard against the wind as it progresses from flower to flower; it rarely settles, preferring to half-hover, half-cling to its support. The related scarce swallowtail *Iphiclides podalirius* is one of the most delightful of all insects to watch in flight. I have the good fortune of being able to visit each year a favourite stronghold of these doughty performers in the hilltop village of Jimena de la Frontera in southern Spain. The village is surmounted by a ruined castle, clinging to the crag tops. The winds swirl furiously around the battlements, providing a benediction for anyone who makes the short climb up from the sultry village streets. Rock martins and swifts flash gleefully over the battered walls and griffon vultures look down imperiously from between their vast canopial wings. None of them deters the scarce swallowtail, which is just as happy to launch into momentary pursuit of the rock martins as it is to engage a rival butterfly in a furious display of acrobatics. In a trice, its pace will drop from a helter-skelter, high-speed swoop to a delicate, inching approach to a flower. Most skilful of all, it will glide effortlessly in circles, wings held in a V-shape. It would be difficult to imagine a more exquisite display of flight in any animal.

92. This photograph of the tiny leaping springtail *Tomocerus* shows the forked tail extending from the end of the abdomen. Before the insect lands, the tail will have been withdrawn into its groove on the underside of the abdomen. Note the strong flexure in the insect's back, which probably reflects the effort involved in increasing fluid pressure within the body cavity to bring about eversion of the tail. The insect is performing a backward somersault, as indicated by the downward bending of the long, whip-like antennae.

· 8 ·

FLIGHT WITHOUT WINGS

There is a group of tiny insects that most of us never notice even though they are sometimes literally beneath our feet. And you need go no further than your own garden. Whenever you disturb neglected rubble heaps, piles of old masonry or overgrown plant-pots you will be evicting not only earwigs, wood-lice, centipedes and spiders but also springtails.

Springtails are denizens of cool, dark places – one of the commonest places you can find them in concentrated numbers is beneath the rotting bark of fallen trees. They are usually drably coloured, and none of them measures more than a few millimetres in length. They easily escape attention, but there may be millions of them in an acre of woodland.

It must be said that on the face of it they have little to commend themselves to the average naturalist – not even wings. Even taxonomists have relegated these tiny creatures to the status of 'primitive insects' – not out of contempt, but because they show a number of features that we would expect to find in the ancestors of modern flying insects. For instance they lack compound eyes, possess only the rudiments of a tracheal system, and show no sign that they ever had wings.

But there is also another way at looking at this question: if an insect lives in the dark it does not need compound eyes or the refined image-making capability that goes with them. Wings would certainly get in the way, and if the insect spends a lot of its time sitting around browsing on microscopic plants and conserving its energy, it does not need a sophisticated tracheal system. So, although the springtail may be defined as primitive, it is also so well adapted to its environment that it is one of the most abundant animals on earth.

Dr S. M. Manton of London University devoted most of a working lifetime to the study of these and other related insects, and her endeavours resulted in one of the most prodigiously and accurately detailed accounts of animal structure ever published. Much of her interest centred on the remarkable 'tail' of the insects, which functions as a springing organ, and she was led to the conclusion that in some species virtually the entire anatomy of the body had been adapted towards the effective functioning of this organ. This seems to be a case of extreme specialization, yet probably no more so than what we find in a kangaroo or a bat. These too have modified the rest of their body

around the organ of propulsion. The main difference is that kangaroos hop and bats fly most of the time, whereas a springtail probably uses its tail only in emergencies. But even if the tail were used only once in the insect's lifetime, and saved it from being eaten by a predator, the investment would have been justified.

The tail, technically known as the 'furca' or fork, is not a real tail at all – when you look at it closely, it is attached to the fourth and fifth segments of the abdomen and not to the end of it. It seems to represent the fused appendages of the fourth segment, a distant echo of the time when the first insects on earth carried 'legs' on the abdomen as well as the thorax. Similar leg-like projections are found along the abdomen of the other main group of wingless insects related to spring-tails, the so-called bristle-tails, which include the silverfish often found slithering about on the bottom of the bath in the early hours of the morning.

The mechanism of the tail
The anatomy of the tail is shown in Figures 28 and 29. It is normally stowed away in a groove or gutter on the underside of the abdomen. When released, the tail springs out

93. The other main groups of wingless insects apart from the springtails are the three-tailed bristle-tails (Thysanura) which includes the familiar silverfish, and the two-tailed bristle-tails (Diplura), one of which, a species of *Campodea*, is illustrated here. *Campodea* is common beneath stones, moss-covered logs and similar moist dark places, and appears to be totally blind.

of the groove, strikes the ground and 'pole-vaults' the insect into the air. On the face of it the whole thing seems to work like a clasp-knife, the gutter being the groove on the knife handle, the tail being the knife blade. Evidently Manton must have had a similar analogy in mind because she concluded that, like a knife blade, the tail is spring-loaded, and held down by a 'catch' ready to be released in an emergency. A catch can indeed be identified, consisting of a tiny conical projection from the surface of the groove called the hamula and this con-veniently engages into the notch between the two arms of the fork whenever it is folded away.

But if you manipulate the tail of an insect that has only recently died, or which has been anaesthetized with a whiff of carbon dioxide, a slightly more complicated picture emerges. This experiment is best done using a pair of watchmaker's forceps and a

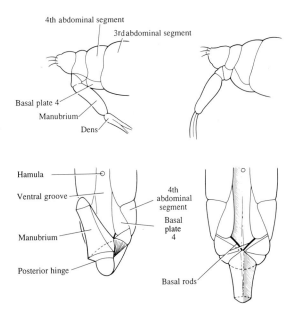

Figure 28. These drawings of the tip of the abdomen in a 'cylindrical' springtail illustrate the structure of the springing organ or furca. The main part of the organ, called the manubrium, articulates with the abdomen via a hinge line, the posterior hinge. The furca is seen from the side in the partly flexed (upper left) and partly extended (upper right) positions. It is normally stowed away in the ventral groove, as the view from below (below left) indicates. In the extended position (below right) the connection between the base of the furca and the basal plate of abdominal segment 4, via the basal rods, can be seen.

binocular microscope. Moving the tail in and out of the groove, you discover that it has two stable positions which it prefers to be in: fully flexed into the groove or fully extended out of the groove. Holding the tail at any position between these extremes, then releasing it, causes it to snap either in or out, depending on its exact starting position. The tail likes to be 'in' or 'out', and is evidently under elastic tension at any intermediate position.

Manton was correct in everything except the final, but important, detail: the tail will spring out of the groove, yes, but only when it has first of all been brought to the thres-hold by some other force. Then, when the tail is roughly halfway out, the spring will finish the job and snap it fully out.

This mechanism might strike you as being unnecessarily complicated, but in fact every reader engages in an action involving the same principle several times a day. It is exactly the principle involved in flicking a light-switch. A switch-lever is spring-loaded to make sure that it is either 'on' or 'off': a switch that was prone to hovering in between would be dangerous and useless. Animals too have developed these switch or 'click' mechanisms. We have already seen the principle at work in the vibration of the insect's thorax during flight (Chapter 2), and on an entirely different scale it occurs in the fetlock joint of a horse.

There are two main reasons why they use click mechanisms. One is the same as that in-volved in the design of an electrical switch: it rules out uncertainty. Even if a springtail had an efficient catch to hold its tail in place, it could never be absolutely sure that the tail wouldn't accidentally 'go off'. This uncer-tainty would always be there if the tail functioned simply like a clasp-knife.

The second reason is that a click mechanism allows energy to be built up gradually in a structure, then released in an explosion. We have already met cases involving the explosive release of energy during the discussion on leaping insects in Chapter 3. What was said there about grass-hoppers applies equally to springtails. The reason for having an elastic spring in the tail

is that it enables energy to be released by the tail at a rate far greater than real muscles could ever achieve. This can be demonstrated if you measure the speed of a springtail as it leaps off the ground. You find that the amount of muscle needed to accelerate the body to such a speed over a few thousandths of a second is about ten times the total weight of the insect! Clearly this is impossible.

But if the insect has even a moderately small muscle which can be used slowly to crank up a spring attached to the base of the tail, and it then releases the spring, the situation becomes very different. Calculations suggest that this 'cranking' phase need only take one or two tenths of a second before the spring is released. Could this be what is happening in the springtail's tail as it flicks out of the groove? During the early stage of extension a muscle actively drives the tail towards the threshold point, and at the same time causes the base of the tail to compress a spring. Once the threshold point is reached, the tail is snapped out at high speed. The cranking phase, equivalent to the finger applying pressure to the switch, could take place in the tenth of a second or so immediately after the springtail senses danger. The rapid extension phase, lasting only three or four thousandths of a second, would then secure its escape.

This all seems to fit into place very nicely until you start looking for the spring. Manton believed she had located it in the form of two rods connected between the base of the tail and the exoskeletal ring, or sclerite, surrounding the fourth abdominal segment (see Figure 28). Each time the tail was folded into the groove after use, the base of the tail rotating inwards forced the rods deeper into the body, deforming them and making them store elastic energy which could then be transmitted to the tail base at the next leap.

In fact, this seems to be the opposite of what the rods do. The function of the rods appears to be to transmit the movement of the base of the tail, during the first phase of tail extension, to the sclerite. For this purpose the sclerite is shaped like a ring with a section cut out, as Figure 29 shows. The rods attach to the edges, or jaws, of the ring and force them apart making them distort the ring and store elastic energy within it. When the base of the tail reaches a critical position in its outward movement, the ring suddenly recoils to its original shape, driving the rods outward at high speed against the base of the tail. So the main source of elastic energy storage seems to be the sclerite, not the rods.

94. This photograph shows a species of tiny (c. 2 mm long) globular springtail *Dycyrtoma ornata*. Like their cylindrical relatives, globular springtails have a forked springing organ stowed away on the underside of the abdomen, and also spin through the air as they leap.

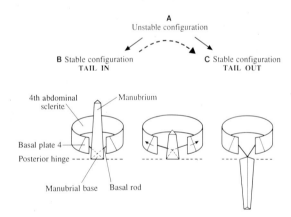

Figure 29. The springing organ of springtails operates on the basis of a click mechanism. The furca has two stable positions, 'in' or 'out', but it is placed under tension in any intermediate position. This tension results from the elastic recoil of the bangle-shaped sclerite of abdominal segment 4. The jaws of the bangle are connected to the base of the tail by the basal rods. If the tail is manually rotated out from the resting position seen on the left to the halfway position seen in the middle diagram, the basal rods force apart the jaws of the bangle. If the tail is now released, the elastic recoil of the bangle will snap the tail either 'in' or 'out' at high velocity. In the living insect the sequence of movements during tail eversion would be **B** (stable) → **A** (unstable) → **C** (stable), as shown by the dotted line.

This model satisfactorily accounts for the bistable or switch-like properties of the tail, but it still leaves unexplained the source of energy that drives the tail out to its threshold point. It is not easy to find a muscle that will do the job. Manton's original drawings show a few muscles attaching to the tail base from within the body cavity, but they are extremely tiny and do not seem fit for the role.

If we look for muscle inside the springtail's body we find plenty of it, but not attached to the tail. It is attached in large quantities immediately beneath the body wall, stretching in long bands between the sclerites. These bands of muscle are perfectly suited to the job of telescoping the segments into one another, and thereby shortening the abdomen. We see similar abdominal 'pumping' movements in insects when they are breathing. This is where the ultimate source of power for tail extension seems to lie.

Rapid contraction of these muscles can telescope the abdomen, pumping up the pressure of the fluid inside it and forcing out the tail like the finger of a rubber glove blown out by air. The beauty of the mechanism is that it allows the combined resources of a relatively large mass of muscle not directly attached to the tail to be concentrated on

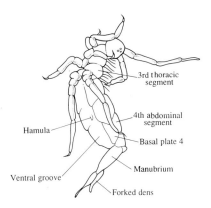

Figure 30. Drawing of the 'cylindrical' springtail *Orchesella villosa* in mid-jump, based on an original photograph. The tail is being retracted into its groove on the underside of the abdomen following the immediately preceding phase of extension. Note the pronounced backward flexure of the head and thorax on the abdomen. This may be due to a 'whiplash' effect following the striking of the tail on the ground, but is more likely to be caused by active contraction of the muscles spanning the segments on the upper side of the body.

driving out the tail as rapidly as possible, thereby priming the spring in readiness for the high-speed extension phase.

Most of the ideas expressed above are based on anatomical observations, but is there any experimental evidence that this is the way the spring works? High-speed photography offers some clues. As photograph 92 shows, when the springtail jumps its back becomes arched strongly backwards like that of a gymnast performing a backward somersault. The back muscles of gymnasts are extremely well developed to allow them to perform such flexures. Extrapolating from the example of the gymnast, it seems likely that what the springtail is doing is contracting the muscles along its back in order to telescope the abdominal segments and drive the body fluids down towards the base of the tail, causing it to flick out. If you look carefully at the photographs, you will see that the antennae of the insect are bent down below its face as a result of the air pressure. If a gymnast had pigtails and you photographed her somersaulting backwards a similar thing would be seen. We can conclude that not only is the springtail leaping upwards, it is also somersaulting backwards.

Modelling springtail jumping on a computer

It turns out that the jumping of springtails has an even more unexpected parallel in the human domain, and one that could have an important application. Imagine a vehicle travelling at high speed along a motorway. It sometimes happens, although fortunately not very often, that the transmission shaft from the gear box to the rear wheel axle comes adrift at its front connection and drops on to the road. The result is that the car, under its own momentum, pole-vaults forwards over the transmission shaft. At the same time, it may also somersault backwards. Clearly the springtail provides the perfect ballistic model for analysing this kind of accident, and on this account alone it would be worth looking at in depth.

Dr Hugh Hunt, of Cambridge University's Engineering Department, recognized the potential applications of the jump of the springtail and set about the complex mathematical problem of modelling it on a computer. The physical ingredients of the model can be derived relatively simply from the fact that the springtail levers its body into the air with a rod that is located at the end of its body. This simple fact in itself immediately distinguishes springtails from almost every other leaping animal. The grasshoppers and crickets that we saw in Chapter 3 for example, attach the hind legs, which are their equivalents of vaulting poles, directly beneath the centre of gravity. The reason why most animals do this is clear: it means that the force projecting the body into the air passes directly through the centre of mass and not in front of or behind it. In either of the latter cases, the force from the legs would make the body spin as it moves through the air. Apart from being a waste of energy, spinning would mean that an animal would never know whether it would land on its head or its feet.

So once the springtail has chosen to put its 'pole-vault' at the end of its body it cannot help but spin as it leaps, and indeed high-speed cinematographic studies have shown that springtails have no particular preference for landing on their heads or their tails. Fortunately, the clinical consequences of an insect weighing in at a thousandth of a gramme landing on its head are by no means as great as those that would follow in the case of a much heavier animal. As far as we know, springtails are not regularly concussed by their leaping efforts, although one imagines there must be occasional cases of mild headache!

Why do springtails spin as they jump?

Springtails come in two main forms: some have globular bodies and some have cylindrical bodies. I was particular interested to see what effect these differences in shape might have on the ballistics of the insects and asked Dr Hunt to design this capability into his model. The abstractions of shape that a mathematician can arrive at are a marvel to behold, and an object lesson to any biologist. Whether the body is round, elliptical or shaped like a sausage, for modelling pur-

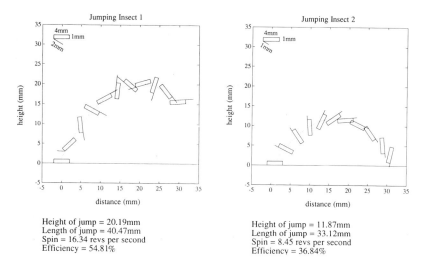

Height of jump = 20.19mm
Length of jump = 40.47mm
Spin = 16.34 revs per second
Efficiency = 54.81%

Height of jump = 11.87mm
Length of jump = 33.12mm
Spin = 8.45 revs per second
Efficiency = 36.84%

Figure 31. A computer simulates the jumping of a cylindrical springtail such as *Tomocerus*. Insect 1 has a tail of 2 mm in length, twice as long as that of insect 2. Both insects jump from left to right and both somersault through the air. Although both insects release the same amount of elastic energy from their tails, insect 1 gains greater leverage and jumps almost twice as high but also revolves almost twice as fast. Spinning represents wasted energy, but ironically it seems to be the price that the springtail has to pay to achieve greater height in its jumping.

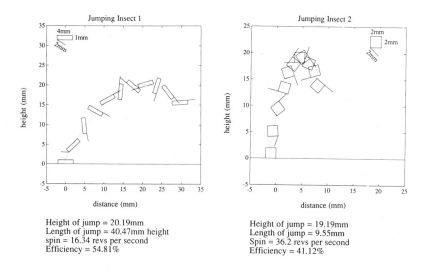

Height of jump = 20.19mm
Length of jump = 40.47mm height
spin = 16.34 revs per second
Efficiency = 54.81%

Height of jump = 19.19mm
Length of jump = 9.55mm
Spin = 36.2 revs per second
Efficiency = 41.12%

Figure 32. The computer model shows how a change of body shape can radically alter the characteristics of the jump in springtails. Both insects have the same body weight and length of tail, but insect 1 is a cylindrical type like *Tomocerus* whereas insect 2 is a globular type like *Dicyrtoma*. Both insects jump through the same height, but insect 1 achieves four times the horizontal distance. Both insects somersault backwards, but the globular springtail spins twice as fast and in so doing appears to waste a lot more energy. As a result, the range achieved is only half that of the cylindrical species.

poses it can all be boiled down to a rectangle with a stick placed at one angle of the rectangle to represent the tail.

Dr Hunt's models confirmed the evidence of the high-speed camera that some species spin through the air at up to a hundred times per second. In the process they waste up to 30 per cent of their leaping energy. We therefore asked the computer what must be done to the design of the body, in order to eliminate this source of wastage. The answer is that the objective can be achieved, but only by having such a severely truncated tail that little height or distance can be gained by the jump. Real springtails seem to have adopted the best compromise, accepting a certain degree of spinning in order to obtain height and distance in their jumping.

It would be gratifying to think that after all the time that had been spent modelling the dynamics of springtail jumping we had gained a definitive answer to this intriguing little problem. However, we have only part of

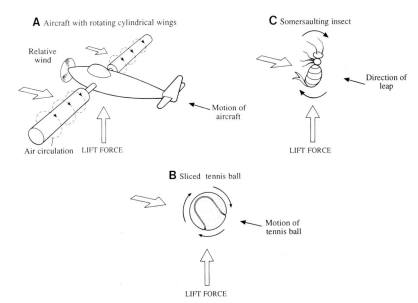

Figure 33. In theory it is possible for an aeroplane to produce lift from cylindrical wings, as long as the cylinders are made to rotate in the direction shown. The rotation of the cylinders produces an air circulation around the wing similar to that induced by a cambered aerofoil. This is known as the Magnus effect. The same effect can be seen in a sliced tennis ball which, because of its rotation, 'floats' through the air. Globular springtails spin rapidly through the air as they jump. Is it possible that, like the backwardly sliced tennis ball, the insect gains 'lift' which helps it to stay fractionally longer in the air?

the answer because, only naturally, we had assumed that spinning is a waste of energy. And this may have influenced our modelling. But what if the springtail has a real use for spinning? It is easy to think of arguments against the spinning. Apart from the question of energy economy, high-speed spinning must impose considerable shearing stress on the organs suspended within the body cavity, including the nervous system.

There is, however, one possible use that I can think of. It stems from the fact that a leaping globular springtail, and these are the ones that spin fastest, could not have designed itself better if it had wanted to emulate the behaviour of a heavily sliced tennis ball. Let me elaborate. A tennis-player applies top spin or back spin to a ball depending on whether he wishes it to drop to the ground more rapidly, or more slowly as the case may be. It is the latter 'floated' delivery that is of interest in the present context. The principle behind the 'floated' tennis ball is well known in aerodynamics and is called the Magnus effect. A ball, or even for that matter a long cylinder (see Figure 33), moving forwards through the air but at the same time spinning backwards around its own axis, generates lift – in other words, it 'floats'. Could it be that, by spinning backwards as it leaps through the air, the springtail gains enough lift to extend the length and duration of its leap, even if by only a fraction of a second? Such an improvement in performance, though slight, might still gain it an advantage over a predator.

We do not know the answer to this problem. The question may simply lead into a dark alley, and we will not know until we have seriously examined it. But by rehearsing the arguments involved in analysing the behaviour of these curious animals, the reader will have gained an idea of the complexity of the problem. More importantly, we begin to see how much common ground there is between activities apparently as remote from one another as flight and jumping in springtails. The idea of 'flight without wings' is still a possibility that remains to be investigated.

95. The only practical way to photograph leaping or flying insects is to trigger a camera automatically by making the body of the insect interrupt a narrow light or laser beam placed in its path. The breaking of the beam triggers an electromagnetic shutter that opens within one hundredth of a second to expose the insect's body to a flash of light. Some insects leap so fast that they evade even this system. The blue-winged grasshopper, *Oedipoda caerulescens*, shown in this photograph displaying 'flash coloration' in its wings could only be photographed using a specially-designed shutter that opens within three-thousandths of a second.

· 9 ·

COPING WITH A NEW CHALLENGE

At the time of writing this chapter I have received a letter from a Dr Giuseppe de Marchi of Milan who, after reading a scientific article that I wrote, '... would like quickly to gain the technical skill to take photographs of flying insect'. I admire Dr Marchi's optimism. 'Quickly' is a word that I dropped from my vocabulary soon after embarking on the same adventure as Dr Marchi's. I was prepared for the fact that the behaviour of insects is utterly unpredictable; but when instrumentation also began to assume a will of its own, despair and distraction became frequent companions.

So it will be with Dr Marchi, unless he has a magic formula. But I am sure he will pre-

vail as long as he remembers that working with live insects, like working with any other animal, requires limitless patience. Results will not come quickly: the photographs in this book represent approximately 1 per cent of my entire endeavour in this area over the last four years. I have spent hours editing out thousands of photographs containing nothing even vaguely recognizable as an insect. Just as often I would find a well-focused 'foot' suspended mysteriously in the upper corner of the picture, its dismembered body having completely eluded the camera.

But the main purpose of this chapter concerns the most recent phase of my work, which is providing a fascinating new challenge. Studying insects in flight requires a considerable amount of gadgetry, both electronic and photographic. Most of this is available technology, but occasionally a point is reached in any project where the technology fails to cope with a new demand, and you have to put on your thinking cap. In my case the challenge to the system came from an unlikely-looking candidate, the frog-hopper *Cercopis vulnerata*. Let me explain.

The sub-order of insects called Homopterans contains many species which are highly specialized jumpers. Most are small in size, such as the frog-hoppers, leaf-hoppers and tree-hoppers, but the sub-order also includes the cicadas, some of which are very large insects. These hopping bugs pose a fascinating puzzle because they leap at tremendous speeds and yet their legs show none of the obvious specializations that we see in grasshoppers and flea-beetles, for example.

The beautifully black-and-red coloured frog-hopper *Cercopis vulnerata* is one of the first 'true' bugs to emerge in British hedgerows in springtime. You have only to look at it to realize that it is designed to move through the air like a bullet. The body has a typical wedge shape, like Formula One racing cars, with a pointed nose that gradually widens behind. The sleekness of form owes much to the smooth, fastened-down wing cases, but once these are opened the streamlining is lost just like the smooth profile of a sports car is lost if the doors are opened.

If you place a *Cercopis* on the back of your hand and prod it into action with your finger you will be impressed by the speed at which it makes its escape. In fact, although you will feel a tiny pulse in your skin as it takes off, you will probably see nothing. If you repeat the exercise several times you will eventually see that at a distance of about half a metre from your hand the leaping insect momentarily reappears into view, as though suddenly halted in its tracks, before proceeding to fly away with an audible buzz of its wings. This sequence of events is very rapid, so you will have to watch carefully.

You may well conclude, as I did when I first looked at this insect, that its escape falls neatly into two stages: a first stage when it leaps rapidly through the air aided by its smooth profile, then a second stage when its wings suddenly open in preparation for flight. The increase in drag caused by the wings opening slows down the body, but only momentarily until the wings start generating power.

The basics of photographing flying insects
I set about trying to confirm this idea by photographing the insect on the point of launch: the question was, were the wing cases closed, or were they beginning to open, as the frog-hopper took off? This is the point at which the technology failed me. To understand the way in which the frog-hopper foiled the system, it is necessary to describe briefly the kind of equipment needed to photograph flying and leaping insects.

The first thing that needs to be said, although it may be obvious to some readers anyway, is that it is no use trying to photograph a flying insect with a hand-held camera. This is because the flight path of an insect is so unpredictable and the speed of human reactions so slow. Even if an insect was flying straight towards the close-up lens of a camera as you held it, and even if it was travelling at only a fast walking pace, you would have less than ten thousandths (one hundredth) of a second to react as it snapped into, then out of, focus. Compared to this, the human eye-to-hand response time is approximately two hundred and fifty thousandths (one quarter) of a second! The insect would have flown another 30 cm in the direction of the photographer's nose even before the signal had left his retina on its way to the brain, and a further 50 cm before his hand had touched the shutter button. Add to that a further delay of at least a quarter of a second in the camera mechanism itself, and you can see that time and speed conspire to make the mission virtually impossible.

The solution is to make the insect photograph itself by using an automated system in which, once the subject breaks an electromagnetic beam (infra-red, white light or laser) it triggers the opening of the camera shutter. Immediately the shutter is open a flash-gun discharges to provide the appropriate illumination for the subject. It is no good relying on the camera's own inbuilt shutter, which is far too slow. A specialized electromagnetic shutter, which will respond almost without delay to the signal from the beam detector, will need to be fitted either in front of or behind the camera lens.

Commercially available leaf shutters have an inbuilt delay of approximately eight thousandths of a second, almost all of which is due to mechanical linkages in the shutter blades. Such a system is capable of taking a picture of a moving object approximately one hundred times faster than a human being could take it and many of the photographs in this book relied on the use of such a shutter. However, it proved woefully incapable of stopping the motion of the frog-hopper! Scores of trials using a conventional electromagnetic shutter resulted in photographs that bore either no image at all or at best an unidentifiable blur. Similar failure attended my attempts to photograph some particularly fast-leaping species of grasshopper and bush-cricket. If I were to stand any chance of success with these exceptionally energetic insects, I decided, I would have to devise a shutter that was capable of opening within two or three milliseconds. This is far beyond the capabilities of conventional electromagnetic shutters.

Some readers might be prompted to ask at this point why I did not dispense with the shutter altogether and simply arrange the system so that, as soon as the insect broke the light beam, the flash-guns discharged. This, however, is totally impractical. Without a shutter the film in the camera would be continuously exposed, so it would only be possible to photograph in darkness. Not only would this be exceedingly difficult for the photographer, but, apart from night-flying moths, it is unlikely that any insects would fly in the dark!

Designing a super-fast shutter

I therefore set about designing my own shutter. I started from the knowledge that most of the opening delay in an electro-

magnetic shutter of the iris diaphragm type is due to the inertia of the shutter blades which, after receiving the driving signal from the solenoid, have to be accelerated from rest to a fully open position. The radial distance travelled by the blades is of the order of 20–30 mm. This is necessary in order to expose the fully diameter of the front element of the lens to the light. Further resistance to the movement of the shutter blades comes from their mechanical linkages and from the fact that they are spring-loaded to ensure that they snap closed again after the opening pulse from the solenoid has ceased.

All three of these physical ingredients of the shutter would have to be minimized in the new design. This could be done by reducing the shutter to a single blade hinged on a frictionless bearing and free of any kind of spring-loading. Moreover, the distance through which the blade moved would have to be kept down to 2–3 mm.

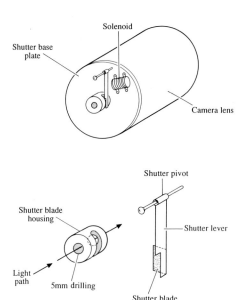

The design finally adopted is shown in Figure 34 and is, on first appearance, a rather odd-looking creature. It consists of a thin metal plate into the centre of which is drilled a 4 mm diameter hole. The plate screws on to the front of the camera lens and the hole therefore controls the light entering the camera. The hole is serving the same

Figure 34. A high-speed shutter. The shutter consists of a single blade carried at the end of a lever which pivots freely at its base. The blade is just large enough to cover the hole in the base plate which functions as the effective aperture of the lens. The shutter blade housing minimizes light entry into the lens when the shutter is in the non-activated state. When activated, the lever, which is made out of a magnetic metal, is drawn to the solenoid, exposing the lens to light coming in through the front hole of the shutter blade housing.

function as a conventional 'between-the-lens' iris diaphragm, and its diameter has been calculated to give an effective F-number of F22, ensuring maximum depth of field. One must be careful to ensure that the inbuilt iris diaphragm of the camera lens is fully opened (to F2.8, F4 or whatever the nominal aperture of the lens may be), otherwise virtually no light at all can get into the lens.

Entry of light into the lens is controlled by a shutter blade consisting of a lever arm freely hinged from a piece of ordinary dressmaker's pin, and carrying at the end a tongue of metal just big enough to cover the hole in the shutter plate. The hole is surrounded by a housing which is light-tight apart from a second hole, 5 mm in diameter, directly in line with the first. A narrow slot in the side of the shutter housing permits the metal tongue of the shutter blade to be interposed between the two holes. The shutter is activated by an electrical pulse delivered to a small solenoid mounted closely alongside the shutter blade lever. This draws the tongue out of the slot, temporarily exposing the lens to the light.

Remember that, in order to reduce the resistance of the shutter blade, it was designed to be free of any spring-loading. Nevertheless it is important that, after the shutter has been opened, the blade returns to its closed position as soon as possible in order to prevent stray light entering the camera. To achieve this rapid return a small pad of rubber, cut from an elastic band, is mounted on the face of the solenoid. This does not interfere with the movement of the lever as it swings out of the shutter housing, but over the final millimetre of its outward journey the lever compresses the pad. Once the electrical pulse to the solenoid has ceased, the rubber pad recoils, sending the blade back into the housing without delay.

Timing is of the essence in the operation of the shutter. The electrical pulse delivered to the shutter solenoid originates from the photocell detecting the light beam as it is broken by the flying or leaping insect. Trials showed that the shutter blade had cleared the housing in just less than three thousandths of a second. A time delay circuit was then designed so that the signal from the photocell, in addition to activating the shutter solenoid, discharged a flash-gun 3.2 milliseconds later, just at the time when the shutter was fully open. The intricacies of this circuitry were worked out by an electronics engineer and fellow conspirator in this enterprise, Andrew Dack, without whose skills nothing could have been achieved.

It came as something of a surprise to me that the whole thing worked. As soon as possible I tried it out on a *Cercopis*, and within minutes of receiving the processed transparencies the story was unfolding. The evidence showed that I had been wrong in my assumption that the wings remained closed for the first part of the jump. In fact they begin to open from the very instant of take-off, as can be seen in photograph 23A.

But the leaping of the frog-hopper was really only the beginning of the challenge. The shutter has opened up new possibilities. The camera can now be pointed towards insects that previously eluded it and, because of their propensities, these are in many ways the most interesting species. The cicada shown in photographs 21A and B and 55A and B, for instance, takes off with remarkable speed: in fact its movements are so rocket-like that, even with a new shutter, I was doubtful of my chances of success.

I am still puzzled by the remarkable performance of frog-hoppers and cicadas. Their legs look ridiculously feeble in comparison with the task for which they are employed. Is there a hidden spring somewhere in the base of the legs? Or do the wings in their first one or two beats generate enough power, possibly by a special mechanism, to accelerate the body to high speed? I do not know the answer to this problem, but at least I am now in a position to pose some of the questions. A moment of triumph, maybe – but the frog-hoppers have still not been tamed. As I conclude this chapter I have to report that several specimens of another frog-hopper recently beaten down from an English oak have sped past my shutter leaving no trace behind! The challenge continues.

FURTHER READING

Dalton, S. (1975), *Borne on the Wind*. London: Chatto & Windus. A beautiful compilation of insects photographed in flight, and a classic of its kind. Its factual content, however, is very limited.

Brackenbury, J.H. (1990), *Insect Flight: the Ultimate Flying Machines*. Australian Natural History. Volume 23, pp. 368–377.

Brackenbury, J.H. (1991), *Insect Origami*. Australian Natural History. Volume 23, pp. 562–569.

The following are more technical in nature:

Bennet-Clark, H.C. (1975), 'The energetics of the jump of the locust', *Journal of Experimental Biology*. Volume 63, pp. 53–83.

Brackenbury, J.H. (1991), 'Kinematics of take-off and climbing flight in butterflies', *Journal of the Zoological Society of London*. Volume 224, pp. 251–270.

Ellington, C.R. (1984), 'The aerodynamics of hovering insect flight', *Philosophical Transactions of the Royal Society of London*. Volume 305B, pp. 1–181.

Rayner, J.M.V. (1979), 'A new approach to animal flight mechanics', *Journal of Experimental Biology*. Volume 80, pp. 17–54.

Weis-Fogh, T. (1975), 'Flapping flight and power in birds and insects, conventional and novel mechanisms for lift production', in *Swimming and Flying in Nature*. Volume 2, pp. 729–762. New York and London: Plenum Press.

Wootton, R. (1981), 'Support and deformability in insect wings', *Journal of the Zoological Society of London*. Volume 193, pp. 447–468.

96. A queen hornet wasp *Vespa crabro*, recently emerged from winter hibernation. Her fat stores now almost depleted, she will begin to search eagerly for food, mainly other insects.

INDEX